The Call of Destiny

Marie-Louise von Franz, Honorary Patron

**Studies in Jungian Psychology
by Jungian Analysts**

Daryl Sharp, Founder and General Editor Emeritus

THE CALL OF DESTINY

An Introduction to
Carl Jung's Major Works

J. Gary Sparks

Library and Archives Canada Cataloguing in Publication

Sparks, J. Gary (John Gary), author.
The Call of Destiny:
an introduction to Carl Jung's major works / J. Gary Sparks

(Studies in Jungian psychology by Jungian analysts; 146)

Includes bibliographical references.

ISBN 9781738738502

1. Jung, C.G. (Carl Gustav), 1875-1961-Criticism and interpretation.
I. Title. II. Series.

BF109.J8 S63 2023   150.19   54092—dc23

INNER CITY BOOKS
21 Milroy Crescent Toronto ON M1C 4B6
Canada
416-927-0355 www.innercitybooks.net

Founder and General Editor Emeritus: Daryl Sharp
Honorary Patron: Marie-Louise von Franz
Publisher and General Editor: Scott Milligen
IT and Production Manager: Sharpconnections.com

INNER CITY BOOKS was founded in 1980 to promote the
understanding and practical application of the work of C.G. Jung.

Cover designed in memory of Daryl Sharp.

Printed and bound in Canada by Rapido Livres Books.

CONTENTS

LIST OF ILLUSTRATIONS

CW refers to *The Collected Works of C.G. Jung*

REMEMBRANCE OF DARYL SHARP

A Personal Remembrance of Dear Friend and Esteemed Colleague
Daryl Sharp, Jungian Analyst: January 2, 1936 – October 8, 2019
Founder and General Editor Emeritus of Inner City Books

He came up to me after I had given a lecture on Wolfgang Pauli to the Jung Foundation of Ontario. "That wasn't half bad for a change," he twinkled. "Why don't you write it up and I'll publish it?" So began a further measure of kinship in my forty-year friendship with, as I like to call him, "The Bard of the North Country Fair" (I write from the US). My first real meeting with the man was decades earlier at Zürich's Bellevueplatz on a sunny spring afternoon when we were both students in the Zürich training program. I was feeling anything but sunny. This was a few weeks after I had arrived in Switzerland to train at the Jung Institute, and everything was going wrong. I was sure I had made a mistake to imagine that I could ever complete the diploma. His path and mine had crossed at the Institute, though we had never exchanged pleasantries. So there, at a busy intersection in the city of Jungian studies, Daryl introduced himself. "How are you?" he continued. "Terrible," I replied, "I'm dying and would be better off jumping into the Zürichsee with a few cinder blocks tied to my feet. There is just no way the study here will ever work out. It just looks impossible." "It's supposed to look impossible," he said. "Otherwise, it won't bring out your best." They were the words I needed to keep going, and I did keep going. A few years later, I had run out of money and was again in despair. Through his connections in Zürich, he energetically made it possible for me to find a position teaching English as a foreign language in the public school system, and thus I was able to successfully finance the remaining years of my Swiss education. His support at critical junctures of my life was no small part of my evolving vocation.

Daryl Leonard Merle Sharp was born in Regina, Saskatchewan. Through his father's accountant position in the Royal Canadian Air Force, the family moved frequently. As a result, Daryl was schooled in six of the Canadian provinces and in due course, graduated from high school in Greenwood, Nova Scotia. He attended Carleton University in Ottawa, receiving a degree in mathematics and physics

7

and one in journalism. Drawn to European writers like Kafka, Rilke, Nietzsche, and Dostoyevsky, Daryl studied at the new University of Sussex in Brighton, where he completed the post-graduate MA degree in literature and philosophy. Moving across the Channel to Dijon, Daryl further immersed himself in the works of Søren Kierkegaard, D.H. Lawrence, and Jean-Jacques Rousseau. While in England, he met and, in time, married Barbara Latham, his wife of 13 years, with whom he had three children. Later, back in England, Daryl encountered the work of C.G. Jung, followed by his studies at the Jung Institute in Zürich from 1974 through 1978. After graduation from the Institute, he returned to Toronto and, with partner Victoria Cowan, his youngest daughter was born. The adoration of all four children for their father, exemplified by the loving stories they relish telling about him has always moved me—the sort of father who took them, when they were of age, to see Crosby, Stills, Nash, and Young, and also Eric Clapton, play Toronto.

In addition to the esteem afforded him by his children, there are other personal reasons why Daryl's friendship touched my core. The support he offered me throughout the training years and then back in North America, his publishing my books, our hanging out together in Indianapolis and Toronto, sipping Scotch with him in his Alvin Avenue home, those quirky e-messages reminding me of the importance of wit and humility all form a deposit of treasured memories.

There are yet further reasons, from a broader horizon, why I sorely miss Daryl Sharp, and those reasons have to do with his role in developing and sustaining Jungian Psychology in North America. I do not believe what Daryl did for Jung's opus in the public eye has been matched in our time by anyone. Salutary in this regard is his supporting, along with Fraser Boa and Marion Woodman, what became the C.G. Jung Foundation of Ontario (public program). He was also a co-founder of the Ontario Association of Jungian Analysts (professional program). Likewise, he served as a training analyst and administrator in the daily grind of those institutions. In addition, the importance of his establishing and serving as the General Editor of Inner City Books, the first Jungian publishing house of its kind on the American continent, deserves special mention. With Inner City, Daryl became not only a trusted and valued publisher, but also, to my feeling, an indisputable cultural creator in our time. A short explanation is in order.

Daryl and I belong to a very elite Jungian club. I am not sure how many of us there are in the world, but as far as I am aware, there are only three members of our club in North America: Daryl, myself, and our colleague in Hartford, Connecticut, Jim Scherer. The club is so specialized that it does not even have a name, so I have affectionately dubbed it with a title myself. I call it the "Marie-Louise von Franz Kicked Our Butt Club." When it came time for our mid-point oral exams in the training process (the Propadeuticum or "Propie") with Dr. von Franz on the interpretations of fairy tales, each of us failed magnificently, demonstrating our (in)ability to interpret unconscious material, and we went down hard in a blaze. To Daryl, von Franz explained, "Mr. Sharp, either you are a ninny and have no business being here, or else you have talents as of yet undiscovered." To Jim, she retorted, "Dr. Scherer, your problem is your American education." I, in the spirit of the club-to-be, was surely not spared: "Mr. Sparks, what you said in the exam was just plain stupid." Ouch.

The same something happened, I contend, to each of us in that humiliating disappointment. We were "invited" to acknowledge our puny recognition of the ways and wiles, the depths and breadths, the language and symbols, the healing intent and destructive passions living in the human soul. Our limited grasp became painfully clear as our mentor gracefully took her turn, fully elucidating the images where we stumbled. Von Franz showed us, face-to-face, in her powerfully honest voice and by her relation to the stories we were to understand, what it takes to comprehend the soul. We felt, in the presence of a master craftsperson, how demanding and delicate it is to discern *feelingly* the kind of imagery we—*Deo concedente*—would be spending our life communicating to the minds and hearts of the suffering persons who came to us for consultation. Where we had stuttered in our rationalistic arrogance and had felt our backs begin to sweat, she could show us, even in tales that looked like the epitome of simplicity, the often unrecognized healing intent of the human condition in which each individual is embedded. We experienced with hurricane force the rigor of a consciousness that must be attained in our future work as analysts if the healing substance of a personality is to have a chance. The party is over, boys, she was pretty much saying; walking into the soul of the other with your own soul requires that you know what you are doing and that you do so with an acute mind and feeling heart.

I hasten to add that as a result of our distressing tumbles, we each resolutely found the way to our better integrity.

It is this integrity of mind and heart that the 145 volumes published by Inner City faithfully serve. The books of Eleanor Bertine, Janet Dallett, John Dourley, Edward Edinger, Barbara Hannah, Esther Harding, Joseph Henderson, James Hollis, Rivkah Kluger, Sylvia Perera, Anthony Stevens, Marie-Louise von Franz, Marion Woodman, and 27 of his own, for example, are now familiar to the wider Jungian public, thanks to the small but mighty staff (Daryl, Victoria Cowan, and Scott Milligen) at his home publishing enterprise. Daryl picked up some things big from those years in Zürich, carried them across the Atlantic, and passed them on to a hungry public seeking, sometimes desperately, to make significance and meaning out of their lives as individuals and as citizens.

Thank you, Daryl.

May we in this current generation continue in the tradition of quality he has so astutely plucked from the essence of Jung's work and has, with an exemplary generosity of spirit, put before us as forever gifts.

Previously published in *Psychological Perspectives*, 63: 142–144, 2020

INTRODUCTION

Carl Gustav Jung was born in 1875 in northeastern Switzerland. When he was four months old, his family moved to a small town by the Rhine Falls, where the river drops markedly in a beautiful and roaring spectacle of nature. The town near Schaffhausen, more or less in north-central Switzerland, was where Jung lived until he was six years old. From there, the family settled in the outskirts of Basel in northwestern Switzerland. Jung studied at the University of Basel, graduating in 1900. After his university studies, he served as a resident at the regional psychiatric hospital, the Burghölzli, in Zürich, remaining there until 1909. He then established a practice in psychiatry in his Küsnacht home along the lake of Zürich, not far from the city.[1]

In 1907 Jung met Sigmund Freud, and a six-year personal and professional friendship ensued. Freud was a generation older than Jung, and Jung was eager to learn as much as he could from Freud's years in the psychoanalytic consulting room. Both men had come upon the importance of previously unrecognized unconscious factors in the etiology and curing of psychological suffering. As Freud worked alone in Vienna and Jung likewise alone in Zürich, it must have been a lonely enterprise to uncover such hitherto unstudied motivations in the human struggle for mental and emotional well-being. Their newly-found friendship would have been a welcome oasis in their singular paths—isolated from mainstream viewpoints on human nature as those paths were. Freud's contributions to Jung's grasp of psychiatry and psychoanalysis were certainly invaluable to Jung, and Jung's friendship meant a great deal to Freud. My supervising analyst in Zürich, C.A. Meier, who was close to Freud while Meier continued psychiatry training in Vienna during the late 1920s and early 1930s, told me how Freud would ask him, on his returns from Zürich, "How is Jung? How is Jung?"[2] In the *Face to*

---

[1] C.G. Jung, *Memories, Dreams, Reflections*, chaps. 1–4.
[2] Dr. med. C.A. Meier was, at Jung's request, the first president of the C.G. Jung-Institut Zürich. The references to Dr. Meier come from my conversations with him during my Zürich training.

Face interview with Jung by the BBC near the end of his life,[3] Jung refused to divulge any of Freud's secrets, saying to the interviewer, "These regards last longer than life." Nevertheless, the association between the two pioneers ended with Jung's publication of his first major work, *Wandlungen und symbole der libido,* in 1911–1912. The English translation of that book carries the title *The Psychology of the Unconscious,* which hardly does justice to the German title. The book in English might have more accurately been entitled *Transformations and Symbols of the Libido.* In the pages to follow, a thoughtful survey of this work is presented. As the exploration unfolds, I believe it will become clear how the two men reached a cul-de-sac in their work together, and the split was inevitable. That inevitability, however, doesn't mean it wasn't painful for both men.[4]

From that point until 1928, Jung went through what I call a "night sea journey."[5] He turned a large part of his attention to his inner dreams and fantasies. He painted the images and calligraphed the texts of those dreams and fantasies in his book *Liber Novus* or *The Red Book.* The publishing of that book in 2009 has drawn so much popular attention, I needn't dwell on it. Suffice it to say that Jung's experiences at that time, and the patterns he saw in his images, shaped the backdrop of Jung's unique understanding of how people emotionally and spiritually heal in a time of crisis. It's also important to remember that Jung began his night sea journey just at the beginning of World War One, which lasted from 1914 until 1918. The loss of Freud's friendship may have left a vulnerability in Jung through which the onslaught of passions and images came barreling down on him from the inside. But to say that this whole period of Jung's life was a reaction to the loss of Freud's friendship (or that Jung became psychotic during this time) as amateur critics are wont to do, just misses the mark. In my view, the chaos and violence of the War—Germany is less than an hour's drive from Zürich—erupted in Jung's psyche as well. The emotions behind what was played out in

---

[3] William McGuire and R.F.C. Hull, eds., "The Face to Face Interview," in *C.G. Jung Speaking; Memories, Dreams, Reflections,* p. 432.
[4] *Memories, Dreams, Reflections,* chap. 5.
[5] In *Memories, Dreams, Reflections,* chap. 6, Jung calls this period of his life "Confrontation with the Unconscious."

the horrific events of those years 1914–1918 on the European Continent Jung confronted in himself. More importantly, he found through his ordeal a pattern of healing in the violent chaos, so Jung's inner recognition during that time are truths that are germane to all of us—still discernible in the hideous violence of our time. Jung's recognition and clarification of those patterns of healing became Jungian psychology.[6]

From 1928 until 1944, Jung's writings intensely concerned communicating and explaining the patterns of healing that he found inside himself as the War had raged all around, both inside and outside himself. He delineated, year after year and with infinite care, the restoring and centering dynamics that he could recognize in the storm. This period of generalized sharing his discoveries and insights at the center of his life's work lasted until 1944, the year Jung suffered a life-threatening heart attack.[7]

During Jung's illness and in a delirium close to death, he saw himself being pulled far from earth. He was ready to take his leave, but his medical doctor appeared to him in a vision. Jung writes that the doctor said he "had been delegated by the earth to deliver a message to me, to tell me that there was a protest against my going away. I had no right to leave the earth and must return."[8]

He returned in response to the summons—clearly, fate was telling him there was more to do. His recovery marks the beginning of Jung's most creative period, from 1944 until his death in 1961. It's during these years that he concentrated on writing the volumes that will make up the bulk of this book. With a second lease on life, he wrote steadfastly, producing succinct and, at times, densely packed, volumes, which were the essence of his views on psychological healing and transformation that he had spent a lifetime distilling.[9]

---

[6] *Memories, Dreams, Reflections*, chap. 6.
[7] Ibid., chap. 7.
[8] Ibid., p. 292.
[9] Ibid, chap. 10.

My intent is to present an overview of how and to what end Jung's work developed into a coherent worldview over the course of his life. I would particularly like to give the reader a feel for Jung's writing at the end of his life as one cogent piece. We will examine each of the major books Jung wrote during his final creative phase, and we will clarify the thematic threads among them as they form a complete and singular tapestry with a solid continuity for psychology and beyond. We can watch each volume add a certain aspect to the overall grasp of what Jung felt we needed to know to complete the consciousness journey—for ourselves and, ultimately, for our time.[10]

The four major volumes I will explore that convey the heart of Jung's psychology reached through a lifetime of psychological inquiry are:[11]

Symbols of Transformation, 1911–1912, 1952 (volume 5 of the *Collected Works*)
Mysterium Coniunctionis, 1955–1956 (volume 14)
Aion, 1951 (volume 9, part 2)
Answer to Job, 1952 (published in volume 11)[12]

The presentation of the book material is not in chronological order. The order reflects, rather, the way in which Jung's late works build on each other. Such an organization of the works, I find, adds lucidity as we go about forming a large and overall picture of Jungian psychology.

---

[10] See Appendix Three for dreams pertaining to each of the works discussed.
[11] I have omitted his *Psychology of the Transference*, 1946 (published in volume 16), from this volume. It draws heavily on *Mysterium Coniunctionis* and investigates complexities of one problematic aspect of therapy, namely the erotic attraction between analyst and analysand, which go far beyond my goal here. Our time with *Mysterium* will acquaint us sufficiently with the symbolism of alchemy to meet the overall purpose of this book. In any case, *Psychology of the Transference* is so overwhelmingly rich that it deserves a separate volume itself. It's the volume Jung dedicated to his wife.
[12] *Memories, Dreams, Reflections*, pp. 403–410.

I assume the reader has some familiarity with the basic terms of Jung's psychology, such as ego, shadow, anima, animus, complex, archetype, personal and collective unconscious, synchronicity, etc. Two terms in the Jungian opus that I will discuss throughout the following pages are *spirit* and *Self*. These deserve special consideration as intricate themes that run through Jung's final works and link the works together. Except for these two terms, I presuppose the reader has basic knowledge of the other concepts just mentioned. We will build on a basic knowledge of Jung to find a grasp of his work that has a view of the whole. Hopefully, the curious reader of Jung can continue their independent reading having some idea of how the pieces they are reading fit into Jung's larger opus.

I have felt inspired to undertake this volume in light of just those independent readers. As I have lectured and presented workshops around the US, Canada, and Europe, participants have expressed their frustration concerning the difficulty of digesting Jung's primary works while attempting to read them on their own or in a small group. There are plenty of introductory secondary texts on Jung that are of real value in communicating his psychology at a beginning level, these students of Jung readily agree. When I suggest tackling the major works that are our agenda with the help of Edward Edinger's study guides to those works,[13] thoughtful readers respond that even Edinger's guides feel above their comprehension. I hope this *Introduction to Carl Jung's Major Works* will address the gap between a study of Jungian psychology at an introductory level and Edinger's study guides to the major works—wonderful segues to Jung's essential sources. I'll call the level of the present volume an "intermediate" one. It will lay the groundwork for further study of each of Jung's last writings and will follow the reader's previous familiarity with one of the readily available introductions to his work. Then, Edinger's guides can more effectively lead the way to comprehending Jung's primary texts, which can be approached with a greater measure of clarity and foundational understanding.

---

[13] Edward Edinger's study guides are noted in Appendix Four.

I next turn to *Symbols of Transformation. Symbols of Transformation*, published in 1952, is a rewrite of Jung's first major volume from 1911–1912, as I mentioned above. The 1952 edition, for our intermediate purposes, contains the essence of the 1911–1912 publication. The 1952 publication is conveniently available and conveys the same flavor as Jung's earlier version—I find with a smoother style that does not sacrifice Jung's earliest points of view.

Citations of Jung's writing are indented without any quotation marks while citations of Jung's writing which include quoted ancient texts or dreams examples are indented with quotation marks. Also, where some paragraphs may contain several references from Jung, I will just note their source in a general way.

Let's dive in.

~

The author has received valuable assistance from friends and colleagues during the writing and publishing of *The Call of Destiny*. I would particularly like to thank Scott Milligen and Dave Sharp for their help with the final manuscript as well as for preparing the text for printing. Sincere thanks are amply due to Lila Markley for her assistance editing and polishing the book's text.

SYMBOLS OF TRANSFORMATION

Symbols of Transformation builds the foundation of Jungian psychology as Jung clarifies his views on psychological healing in contrast to those of psychoanalysis. While writing the book, he is still somewhat under the sway of Freud, whom he met in 1907 and studied and worked closely with until 1912. Jung's mature ideas will subsequently build on the foundation laid by *Symbols of Transformation*, which is unique among Jung's works due to its admixture of ideas. At the point of writing this book, Jung really isn't Jung yet. He doesn't fully become Jung, so to speak, until 1928, when his inner ordeal comes to a conclusion and, from there, he begins to clearly form and express his own unique standpoint.

Jung interprets a text by an American woman, Miss Frank Miller, in *Symbols of Transformation*. Miss Miller was a student at the University of Geneva in Switzerland. She recorded her fantasies, dreams, and poetry in her journal while en route to Europe. These were published, quite independently of Jung—Jung had nothing to do with this—by a man named Théodore Flournoy.[14]

After returning from Europe, Miss Miller had a schizophrenic break.[15] Jung came across the material published by Flournoy, and he investigated several pages of her journal to show the psychological process going on in Miss Miller as manifested in her journal writings.

There are levels to the book. Part of the book's intent is for Jung to analyze and understand Miss Miller's journal writings, and part of the book is about her unconscious material. This is not the larger import of the book, however. The larger purpose of the book is to use those writings to show how Jung understands what psychologically happens inside human beings at certain points of their lives. His purpose is to contrast his way of understanding psychological attraction with Freud's conceptions.

---

[14] Historical details come from C.G. Jung, *Symbols of Transformation*, *The Collected Works of C.G. Jung*, vol. 5, pp. xxviiif.
[15] Ibid.

Another aspect of the book is that Jung wrote on two levels in a further sense. Again and again, he literally refers to Freud's ideas. Then he refers to the value of Freudian psychology as providing us with metaphors. Sometimes Jung accepts the literal value of Freud's work; at other times, he reacts to Freud's writing as metaphor—symbolically understanding what Freud took literally. This is a crucial distinction.

In his interpretive agenda, Jung never totally throws out Freud in his work. He says, on the contrary, that Freud's work is true at times on a certain level; understood a certain way, it makes sense. The way he understands Freudian theory may vary from practical instance to instance.

The Book

The following two quotes are from a book called *Analytical Psychology: Notes of the Seminar Given in 1925.* In that seminar, Jung talks about the writing of *Symbols of Transformation*:

> (Miss) Frank Miller, an American student at the University of Geneva, wrote a memoir describing her fantasies, 'Some Instances of Subconscious Creative Imagination,' published (in French) in *Archives de psychologie* (Geneva, vol. V, 1906) with an introduction by the psychologist Théodore Flournoy, who was treating her.[16]

Jung writes:

> As a matter of fact, Miss Miller did afterwards become entirely deranged. During the war I had a letter from the man who was Miss Miller's doctor in America, telling me that my analysis of her fantasy material had been a perfectly correct one, that in her insanity the cosmogonic myths[17] touched upon had come fully to light. Also Flournoy, who had her under observation at the time I first read her material, told me that my analysis had been correct. There was such a

---

[16] C.G. Jung, *Analytical Psychology: Notes of the Seminar Given in 1925,* p. 24, n. 18.

[17] Myths about world creation.

tremendous activity of the collective unconscious that it is not surprising that she was finally overcome.[18]

In the foreword to *Symbols of Transformation,* he likewise writes the following:

This material was originally published by my respected and fatherly friend, the late Théodore Flournoy... I had the great satisfaction of hearing from his own lips that I had hit off the young woman's mentality very well. Valuable confirmation of this reached me in 1918, through an American colleague who was treating Miss Miller for the schizophrenic disturbance which had broken out after her sojourn in Europe. He wrote to say that my exposition of the case was so exhaustive that even personal acquaintance with the patient had not taught him 'one iota more' about her mentality. This confirmation led me to conclude that my reconstruction of the semi-conscious and unconscious fantasy processes had evidently hit the mark in all essential respects.[19]

Two Kinds of Thinking

In the chapter "Two Kinds of Thinking," not only are we learning new material, but we are presented with a new way of thinking about experience. What is Jung's method, and why is it his method? It is critical to understand from the onset the what and why of his method; otherwise, we think he is talking in circles. He *is* talking in circles, but he is talking in circles for a reason.

A story I heard in my training sums up what Jung is driving at in "Two Kinds of Thinking."

A teacher of mine was a British fellow who was an Oxford-trained linguist. Right out of college, he took a job on the district commissioner's staff in Basutoland. Before 1966, Basutoland was the name of the country now known as Lesotho. Currently Lesotho is an independent country within South Africa; at the time of my teacher's

---

[18] *Analytical Psychology*, p. 28.
[19] *Symbols of Transformation*, p. xxviii, cf. par. 46. (Jung's *Collected Works* generally designate references by paragraph number, to sync the references across the German and English editions.)

employ, it was a British protectorate within the country of South Africa. My teacher, being a linguist, learned the Basuto language. He reported in a lecture at the Jung Institute in the middle 1970s an event in which he was talking to the Basuto chief. He asked the chief if he were able to describe the difference between his own (African) people, and people with European ancestry. What is the difference between white people and, as they called themselves, brown people? This was the question my teacher put to the chief.

The chief replied that such a comparison was quite easily made. He continued, "You think in thoughts, and we think in pictures."

Jung's approach to the psyche returns to the original thought processes of human society that think in pictures. Jung, in his deepest work, proceeds not logically but imagistically, which is very much like learning another language. I have found that learning another way of understanding is frustrating at times, but in the long run, retraining my mental processes is well worth the effort. For example, with linear thinking, true statements only have to be logically consistent. With picture thinking, true statements let the reality of experience communicate all its nuance, complications, richness, and perhaps danger. Picture thinking understanding is *guided* by the images that are spontaneously generated by dreams and fantasies— away from the rules of logic as a standard. The image guides the understanding away from arid strictures of logic. It's the only way to fully understand *emotional* experience.

There are practical differences between linear and picture thinking. In normal logic, the mind goes from point A to point B to point C. That is how our minds have been trained through our Western education. With symbolic thinking, the mind does not go in a straight line. Instead, the mind circles around a common image. Jung starts with an image; we'll take the sun, for example. He describes the sun and sun worship in the Near East as dominated by a variety of gods— Osiris, Tammuz, Attis-Adonis, and so on. Then he continues that discussion under the image of fire since the light and heat of the fire can evoke the heat of the fiery sun. Soon he's talking about heroes because gods of the sun have heroic aspects. He next discusses

20

several heroes in considerable depth. Our rational mind protests and clamors, "How in the world did we get from the sun to fire to heroes?" The answer is that the various images contain a particular theme, such as the strength and potency of the heroic attitude in the hero example. All of the images refer back to the central point of the hero and the strength of the hero. The link is not linear but thematically circular. Symbolic or picture thinking is also called "cluster thinking" or "associative thinking." Our understanding works by way of clusters—seeking images with similar themes to explicate each other. We associate to a central image and let relevant tangential images, with a theme similar to the image we start with, contribute to our overall understanding.

This symbolic thought process is the way the dream expresses its messages to us. Clarifying the distinction between the linear mind and the picture, or symbolic mind, is what Jung wants us to understand in his chapter "Two Kinds of Thinking."

"The Hymn of Creation"

Three telling texts in Miss Miller's memoirs are discussed by Jung and illustrate the importance of symbolic thinking.

The main theme in "The Hymn of Creation" is a central one in the book. Put in the most minimal terms, Miss Miller has an erotic feeling, and she begins talking about God the Father. Jung is trying to comprehend how we are to understand that she is probably dealing with a sexual fantasy, and what she talks about is a father image (God the creator in the Book of Genesis). Jung will develop his own way of understanding that juxtaposition.

Miss Miller writes in her journal on the ship to Geneva:

> "One of the officers, singing at night as he stood watch on deck, had made a great impression on me and had given me the idea of writing some words that could be fitted to his melody."[20]

---

[20] Ibid., par. 59.

This is the final version of the poem she creates in response to being impressed by the singing officer. She says that the poem was an instance of "subconscious creative imagination." She "observed" it inside herself instead of it being consciously conceived.[21]

> "When the Eternal first made Sound | A myriad ears sprang out to hear, | And throughout all the Universe | There rolled an echo deep and clear: | 'All glory to the God of Sound.'

> "When the Eternal first made Light, | a myriad eyes sprang out to look, | And hearing ears and seeing eyes, | Once more a mighty choral took: | 'All glory to the God of Light!'

> "When the Eternal first gave Love, | A myriad hearts sprang into life; | Ears filled with music, eyes with light, | Pealed forth with hearts with love all rife: | 'All glory to the God of Love!'"[22]

The detail that Jung explores at considerable depth is the relationship between Miss Miller being impressed by a handsome Italian shipmate and her fantasy of the father god of creation, which ensues from that impressive moment echoing the creation story in Genesis.

Two Interpretations

Jung writes:

> When an impression is denied conscious recognition it reverts to an earlier form of relationship.[23]

Jung's statement is an echo of the Freudian position. The classical Freudian interpretation of Miss Miller's experience would be that she had an attraction to the man, but that attraction wasn't conscious. The energy that would have gone into fulfilling the attraction falls back into the individual and activates the early form of relationship with a man—namely her father. The energy thus in the family constellation, in an unhealthy individual, remains stuck "back there." The early

---

[21] Ibid., p. 447.
[22] Ibid., par. 61.
[23] Ibid., par. 62.

form of relationship keeps the energy away from the present and away from moving forward in the future to a complete relationship with a partner. Miss Miller exemplifies the Freudian perspective as she writes a poem with the energy once evoked by the shipmate—rather than recognizing the urge to connect with another human being. There is no way that her interest in the man will lead her further into life and love. In the Freudian interpretation, the poem was a substitute wish fulfillment of her desire for that man. The images in our unconscious, for classic psychoanalytic theory, are substitutes for fulfilling desire. In sum: images from the unconscious are substitutes.

Jung, by contrast, develops his alternative interpretation:

> The idea of a masculine Creator God is apparently derived from the father-imago, and aims, among other things, at replacing the infantile relation to the father in such a way as to enable the individual to emerge from the narrow circle of the family into the wider circle of society.[24]

In imagining this situation from a Jungian viewpoint, the woman has an attraction, and her energy is moving toward that attraction, but she does not greet the guy who is holding her interest. Instead of reaching out to him, she writes a poem. The energy for the man does not go to the object of her desire, and that energy falls into the unconscious, where it activates the image of her earliest experience of a man—her father. The poem is an expression of her original energy transformed into a cultural creation by the father image, which received the energy to begin with and then redirected the energy to Miss Miller's poetry.

Jung, so far, sounds a lot like Freud. But for Jung, the *image of the father is merely a means, a language, by which a symbol is created for her.* Rather than a substitute for her desire, the poem actually takes the energy of the desire, the energy that she didn't deal with, and reframes the energy for her in another form, *for the purpose of taking her energy into the future.* That's fundamental for Jung. In other words, *images from the unconscious are bridges to transform*

---

[24] Ibid., par. 63.

energy toward the future; they are not mere substitutes for desires unrecognized in the past.

For Freud, images point back to the past. For Jung, they point toward the future.

The Aesthetic Obstacle

Jung, like Freud, recognizes that Miss Miller is blocked. For Jung, she gets stuck in life (her prelude to schizophrenia). She becomes fascinated with the father image, expressed in the poem, rather than understanding what the image means, namely to point her to something new in her life. For Miss Miller, this lack of understanding will end up becoming pathological because she has no means to digest the message to herself from her creation. The nature of the process of creating the poem is healthy; the problem is that she does not know how to receive its message. For Freud, the whole process of the poem's creation is a pathological process. For Freud, we don't know what we really want; the energy activates a substitute image for what we really want but are unaware of; that substitute image is to satisfy the original and disregarded longing. But it never really does. For Jung, the process of creating the poem conceived from the father image isn't substituting for anything. It generates the possibility of future life if the creation that comes out of the experience *is understood and its meaning put into practice.*

Miss Miller's poem does not give her insight into its meaning because she stays fascinated only by the *aesthetic appreciation* of the poem. She doesn't recognize how the poem contains a symbol and, consequently, what she is to learn from this experience. In the long run, she gets stuck in this experience, like a Freudian would argue. But the production of the poem is not the problem; the problem is *not asking any questions about what is happening to her.* She becomes dazzled by what she should interpret. She then slowly removes herself from reality through being dazzled by her experience and the poem. It bears stressing; Jung does not want to say the presence of the poem is a problem; her attitude toward the poem is insufficient. She marvels but does not understand.

24

The Storehouse

As another point of comparison, for Freud, the father image is in Miss Miller's mind because of her relationship with her father. Jung says, on the contrary, that the father image is an intrinsic component of human nature that we are all born with. For Freud, the images in the unconscious are from past personal experience—not so for Jung. Jung understands the inner images as already within us or, more precisely, as inner possibilities already within us for the creating images. That would be the collective unconscious, the storehouse of capacities to produce the imagery that belongs to human beings.

In Jung's words:

> Whoever introverts libido, i.e., withdraws it from the external object ... digs up from the treasure-house of memory those images glimpsed long ago ... .[25]

The father theme, Jung emphasizes, is not necessarily about Miss Miller's personal relationship with her father. The paternal theme comes from the treasure house of images; the father is simply one form of those images.

Teleology

Ultimately, the images pointing to the future that emerge, as in the case of Miss Miller, are there to show us our genuine goal in life:

We must take that moment as foreshadowing a future life-aim.[26]

The "moment" is the moment of the poem's creation where the image manifests to her.

"Foreshadowing a future life-aim" is what Jung means by a symbol that points to the future— the future that it points to has to do with revealing the genuine and true path of our life.

---

[25] Ibid., par. 134.
[26] Ibid., par. 78.

To continue in Jung's words:

> As we have seen, the religious hymn unconsciously produced by Miss Miller appears in place of the erotic problem. It derives its material for the most part from reminiscences which were reactivated by the introverted libido. ... I would ... prefer to find out the *meaning and purpose* of the apparently devious path followed by the libido, and of the apparent self-deception.[27]

The "introverted libido" is the energy that did not flow out to the singing sailor.

His keywords are "meaning" and "purpose." Concerning Miss Miller's father image and its expression in a poem, Jung notes that the creation of the image expresses a:

> teleological orientation in which the cause anticipates the goal.[28]

Teleology comes from the Greek word "telos," which means goal; thus, teleological means "goal-directed." Those few words are a mouthful and introduce an entirely new orientation into psychological analysis. When an experience is teleological, the case is not that the past is influencing the present. With Miss Miller, for example, the future is causing the father imagery to present itself by virtue of the symbol-creating process. The past isn't seen as causing the present; it's more like the future is seen as causing the present.

There is more to say on purpose:

> The intelligent character of this unconscious activity can hardly be denied. ... A man's spiritual vocation in the widest sense ... [is] thrust upon him ... by the unconscious.[29]

Jung steps back from what he's been saying and declares that this process of symbol formation is the one that really tells us who we are. Who we are is something that is given to us through these

---

[27] Ibid., par. 90. [emphasis added]
[28] Ibid., par. 95.
[29] Ibid., pars. 98f.

experiences. We create ourselves insofar as we accept what is given, and we make it real. But we don't create ourselves in the sense that we just think something up and put it into reality. Authentic personhood for Jung is discovered and then created. To consider the kind of experiences that Miss Miller is having as pathological and as wish-fulfillment and as substitute expressions lames the whole future-creating capacity of our inner life that is trying to communicate to us who we are and where we are going.

"The Moth to the Sun"

Miss Miller writes another poem. Jung's interpretation will continue to be mindful of the theme of the previous poem. Here are the first two lines, which themselves say a lot. The poem is entitled "The Moth to the Sun."

> "I longed for thee when I first crawled to consciousness, | My dreams were all of thee when in the chrysalis I lay."[30]

The poem goes on from there. I've just captured the essence of it in these two lines.

Miss Miller, as the title of the poem shows, is putting herself in the place of a moth who is longing for the sun.

In the poem, Jung recognizes the very same dynamic as in the previous instance where the young woman unknowingly longed for the helmsman and ended up producing an image of god in her poem. Here the moth longs for the sun the way Miss Miller was longing for that man and, by extension, for a god-figure. This second poem is another text in which Jung sees the very same dynamic as in the first poem. The attraction is to an image of divinity symbolized by the sun. In the earliest of mythologies, the sun is quite typically the male god; hence, Jung makes the correspondence between the sun and a divinity by implication just as he noted the god reference in the first poem. In both of Miss Miller's poetic creations, a longing for a male divinity is couched between the lines of her verse—in different

---

[30] Ibid., par. 116.

images, it is true, but the symbolic mind recognizes the thematic consistency.

The importance of this distinction is that the nature of the desire remains constant even though the object of the desire is different. Miss Miller has been longing for a man, for a god, for a sun. Jung's symbolic position holds that it doesn't matter if the objects of the longing are so different because what's important to Jung is the longing itself. The nature of the energy that is motivating her longing is not the point. It doesn't matter that it is a sexual longing. It isn't the quality of the experience that interests him—it is the quantity of energy in the experience.

We are not to succumb to the temptation to confuse the language and the message. Whatever the language is doesn't determine what the message is. No matter the form of this experience, it may have a goal that has nothing to do with its form. We may have a sexual feeling, and that feeling may not be about relationship. It may be sexuality is the language used to express something of our future that could have to do with writing a book or getting a new job or learning a new skill—or finally and fundamentally coming to recognize, coming to affirm, who we are and why we are on this earth.

Where does the energy want to go? This is the question to ask in these moments. Regardless of the form in which energy has appeared to us, where does it want to go? When the goal that it is pointing to is reached, the goal that has been reached may have no semblance to the form in which the goal first presented itself to us in an image.

I hasten to add that Jung isn't trying to overthrow Freud's viewpoint as the basic causal model sometimes does apply. In other words, sometimes, if we dream of our father, the issue may be our relationship to our father. But in other circumstances, a dream of our father may be a symbol for a part of our energy that is seeking to realize a personal goal in the development of our talents, our gifts, our overall life orientation, and our ultimate life's meaning. Jung feels this is the case for Miss Miller. Discerning on what level a dream or fantasy image applies for the dreamer is a large part of the sometimes complicated art of Jungian work, which we Jungians must sign up for as we find our way through the images of our unconscious.

The Sun Hero

Now Jung's symbolic or cluster or associative thinking progresses from the creator god, to sun symbolism, to the image of light, and then to figure of sun heroes. Jung clarifies:

> I mention these images in order to show how the light-symbolism gradually develops ... into the figure of the sun-hero.[31]

A particular instance of "these images," namely the image of the sun-hero, would be expressed in the Osiris cycle.[32] I'll linger with sun heroes because now we start looking at the fact this god that we have talked about in the first poem and the sun that we've talked about in the second poem, are—from the symbolic and emotional point of view—really two different forms of the sun hero. Jung will talk at great length about the psychological meaning of the hero in Miss Miller's imagination.

Jung says:

> Under the symbol of "moth and sun" we have dug deep down into the historical layers of the psyche, and in the course of our excavations have uncovered ... the sun hero ... who ... revolves round the earth ... .[33]

---

[31] Ibid., par. 158.
[32] See below.
[33] *Symbols of Transformation*, par. 164.

The Mother, Death and Rebirth

Jung turns to rejuvenation to:

> [the sun hero ... who ... revolves around the earth] ... and who rises
> again *in rejuvenated splendor* to give light to new generations. For him
> the dreamer longs with her very soul, for him the "soul-moth" burns her
> wings.[34]

"Rises again in *rejuvenated splendor*" marks that the chain of
associative thinking has evolved from sun to hero and then from hero
to death and rebirth.

> The ancient civilizations of the Near East were familiar with a sun-
> worship dominated by the idea of the dying and resurgent god—Osiris,
> Tammuz, Attis-Adonis, Christ, Mithras, and the phoenix.[35]

Because of the symbolic link between sun and hero, Jung looks at the
role of heroes, sun heroes, in pre-Christian and slightly post-
Christian myth—for example, Osiris (Egyptian), Tammuz
(Sumerian—Iraq today), Attis (Turkey today), Mithras (Roman).
These gods shared in various degrees three characteristics. They all
were connected with the sun. They all were lovers of their mother. In
that, they were killed, and then they were reborn. Jung has brought
into the sun-hero discussion two elements: *the relationship to the
mother and death and rebirth.*

Keep in mind Jung's chain of symbolic thinking: sun–hero–death and
rebirth–destructive relationship to the mother. She, or some version
of her, kills her son, and he is later reborn.

---

[34] Ibid. [emphasis added]
[35] Ibid., par. 165.

30

There are many variations on the motif of the life and death of the sun hero. Jung spends chapters discussing the fine point of the heroes' differences. Osiris is an illustrative example. (See figure 1.) Osiris is an Egyptian God. He gets into a fight with his brother, who kills him and throws him in a coffin. The coffin floats down the Nile to the Mediterranean and floats to the coast of what today would be Lebanon. There the coffin comes ashore, a tree swoops it up, and Osiris becomes the tree. The king sees this pretty tree and makes the tree a column in his castle. (See figure 2.) That is how Osiris gets to be a column. Osiris is dead, but he is wrapped up in the tree (the tree is a frequent mother symbol throughout early world mythology). His wife, Isis, goes on a hunt for him, finds him, rescues him, and brings him back to life. Then Osiris gets in another fight with his brother, who kills him again. This time Osiris' brother chops Osiris up into fourteen pieces and throws the pieces into the Nile. Isis goes in search of him

Figure 1

Figure 2

31

again. She finds thirteen of the fourteen pieces and puts him back together, although she can't find his phallus. She remakes a phallus for him and conceives a child on the corpse. She gives birth to Horus, who then slays his father's murderer. Horus represents the reconstituted sun, full of power and vigor.[36]

In those early myths, the hero is just beaten up and then brought back to life. And he is passive. Jung shows us that as those myths develop historically—from ancient Egypt, through the civilizations of Mesopotamia, and through the Roman Era—the hero gets more active. The hero doesn't just get beat up, he fights and is killed in a heroic battle, but he is still killed. By the time we get to the Babylonian period, for example, he is not killed. He devours and kills the would-be slayer. The basic idea in those myths is the death and rebirth of the hero as well as the connection between the hero and a maternal figure.

At this point, there is a significant conclusion to draw that has been hovering in the background for some time. What is Miss Miller longing for? And the answer is her rebirth.

We will be looking at the hero as Miss Miller's capacity to turn back to herself, to lose her current orientation (death theme of the myths), and to create a new orientation and find a new basis for her life (rebirth of the hero).

Jung's position has been that her experience on the ship is not about sex or power. On the contrary, the erotic moment is about rebirth. The meaning of her creation poem and her moth poem is that she longs for her own capacity to turn back to herself *and to change*.

The Chiwantopel Obstacle

Jung's discussion will evolve toward the questions of what it means for Miss Miller that her vision is really about death and birth; what the hero is trying to tell her; what it means that her heroes are

---

[36] Ibid., pars. 349–374.

destroyed by the feminine, and how an analyst might communicate to her what she needs to understand at this point in her life.

As we have seen, Miss Miller is transfixed in the beauty of her poetry and never asks what it means. But we will see if there is more to it. The last text that we will talk about from her is entitled "Chiwantopel, a Hypnogogic Vision." It reads as follows:

> "Suddenly, the apparition of an Aztec … with a head-dress … . The name was 'Chi-wan-to-pel.' The figure of Chi-wan-to-pel comes up … on horseback … . An Indian … creeps forward stealthily, making ready to shoot an arrow at Chi-wan-to-pel, who bares his breast to him in an attitude of defiance; and the Indian, fascinated by this sight, slinks away and disappears into the forest."[37]

The slinking away of the Indian is the bad news, worse news than the aesthetic seduction Jung has observed. He has established that the real meaning of the hero is the death and rebirth theme. But here, rather than the ability to die and let the old pass, instead we have an arrogant display. That is where Miss Miller again short-circuits herself. The presence of this image of arrogant display has nothing to do with repressed wishes in the Freudian sense. The image reflects Miss Miller's infantility in being unwilling to consider who she is internally. The unwillingness comes at a high price. For Jung, it's the death and rebirth process that presents us with who we are, the teleological function of the unconscious already mentioned. Jung's viewpoint is unique.

Stressing the indispensability of symbol foundation in the hero's fall and rise, Jung writes that consciousness is

> in danger of being led astray by its own light and of becoming a rootless will o' the wisp, [that] longs for the healing power of nature … .[38]

The healing power of nature would be this symbol-producing process. This is what we connect with in Jungian analysis so that we

---

[37] Ibid., pars. 251, 266, 273, 420.
[38] Ibid., par. 299.

don't just choose to be anything, but we are able to choose the essential and given potential for our lives. This is what grounds our identity in the deepest sense, against all the foolish and irrelevant choices that we make when we don't really consider our deeper direction and meaning.

Stressing the instinctual aspect of this grounding, Jung observes:

> It is not possible to discuss the problem of symbol-formation without reference to the instinctual processes, because it is from them that the symbol derives its motive power.[39]

It is important that our guiding symbols take root in the biological realities of our lives, in the wants and needs and longings of our lives that, in time and with conscious attention, evolve into symbols that show us the genuine way to live.

In this context, Jung continues to discuss how the process of finding the true path in life from the dialogue with symbols from the depths went wrong for Miss Miller. It was her wrong attitude to the inner guiding process—of which death and rebirth were a part—that had a contributing effect to her problem in life, the psychotic episode that awaited her in time.

> We now understand what it was that turned against the naval officer: it was Miss Miller's spirituality, which, personified by the Aztec, was far too exalted for her ever to find a lover among mortal men. ... She will discover only later what the unconscious wants, and this will assert itself either as a change of life style or as a neurosis or even a psychosis.[40]

The symbolic process in Miss Miller went wrong because Chiwantopel, another form of the hero, is something that she identifies with. Rather than seeing him as a symbol for her to go through her own process of growth and contemplating his *meaning* in guiding her through her own process of transformation, a person such as Miss Miller would begin comparing other people to

---

[39] Ibid., par. 338.
[40] Ibid., par. 273.

Chiwantopel as an inner presence. She compares others to an ideal she has herself not realized. The symbolic process, rather than guiding her, actually ends up isolating her.

However, by contrast:

> If the conscious mind now succeeds in interpreting the constellated archetype in a meaningful and appropriate manner, then a viable transformation can take place.[41]

This is what does not happen in Miss Miller's case.

The Hero Myth and Incest

What elements make up the life of the hero? How does the hero play a role in psychological growth that Miss Miller so critically needs at this point in her life? We return to Osiris for a glimpse into the answer.

Jung observes:

> The fate of Osiris is explained: he enters into the mother's womb, into the coffer, the sea, the tree, the Astarte column; is dismembered, put together again, and reappears in his son … .[42]

Through the reference to the mother's womb, which is the symbolic reference of the chest he was thrown into, Jung discusses the psychology of incest.

Freud, if you remember, put incest, the regressive relation between child and parent, at the center of psychological issues—the longing of the son for the mother, the Oedipus complex, in other words, and the longing of the daughter for the father, the Electra complex. That imagery in the form of the mother's womb now appears in this part of Miss Miller's symbolic process. As already stressed, the Freudian interpretation says that the person having this imagery in their dreams

---

[41] Ibid., par. 351.
[42] Ibid., par. 361. The coffer is the chest he was thrown into. The column is from the tree he was absorbed into.

is in an unhealthy and regressive substitute for real life. They are going back to mommy or daddy, or perhaps they never left mommy or daddy because they can't face life.

Jung's position, of course, is quite different. The incest motif is an integral part of the hero cycle because when the hero is killed, he goes back to a mother image. Very often and prior to that, he is his mother's lover. Jung first agrees with Freud. Incestuous imagery can sometimes be a psychological symptom of literal regressions in the parent-child relationship. However, Jung soon departs from that literal viewpoint and recognizes that incest imagery can be a symbol, a metaphor for the hero's turning back to the unknown part of himself symbolized by the mother, which we call the unconscious.

For Jung, the death of the hero and his descent into the incestuous maternal realm means, on the metaphorical psychological level, our interest going down into the depths of ourselves. Why is it symbolized as incest? Because like is uniting with like when we are uniting with ourselves. And this like uniting with like can be experienced as disgusting. It can feel as disgusting to probe into our inner personality as it is to contemplate the possibility of physical incest with our parents.

A disgust has to be overcome when it comes to the inner journey. Everything in us, at this point, will fight the inner gaze because we are taught from day one to get our energy out there in the world and to make a difference in the world. In analytic efforts, we are turning our energy inward and facing ourselves, which at first, feels like a betrayal of all our social values.

Jung certainly recognizes that incest imagery in dreams, for example, can point to a literal issue in our life that we are still too close to our parents. That is, it can alert us to a psychological enmeshment with our parents. Of course, incest imagery can have to do with literal sexual abuse. Or, incest imagery can have nothing to do with either of those. It can be a metaphor for joining with ourselves as we intensely focus on understanding our inner images, thoughts, emotions, etc. That's how Jung understands the incest motif, in the best sense, that we find in the hero myth. The hero is not only about death and rebirth. In the death phase, there is a descent into the maternal realm of the unconscious—maternal because this process gives a metaphorical birth to us along the way of our life just as our biological mother physically birthed us at the beginning of our biological life.

The discussion of the vagaries of the hero myth—its incestuous imagery, its death and rebirth themes—goes on for quite a while. The development of the hero myth in *Symbols of Transformation* continues for well over a hundred pages.[43] Jung surveys a familiar list of hero myths in world culture from Ra and Osiris (Egypt), to Gilgamesh (Assyria), to Marduk (Babylonia), to Mithras (Roman), to Christ, to the Hiawatha legend (Native American), and to Wagner (German). Appendix One lists these heroes and the references in Jung's texts to them. For our purposes, digesting the main pattern of the hero, such as is expressed in the Osiris myth, is sufficient. The curious reader, who may wish to examine the vicissitudes of the life of the hero as it is presented in world mythologies, may find the appendix useful.

It is important to remember that the incest theme can be symbolized in many different ways, starting with a purely passive hero figure to a very active hero who slays the dragon. In the latter case, slaying the dragon would be analogous to Osiris' falling into the ocean; however, that "falling in" would not be a falling at all, but a conscious choice.

Jung puts the latter case this way:

> The fight with the "nocturnal serpent" accordingly signifies conquest of the mother … .[44]

---

[43] Ibid., from paragraph 340 to 570. See Appendix One.
[44] Ibid., par. 375.

Another Obstacle, the Error of Chiwantopel

For Miss Miller, Jung has some important commentary. Where the heroic pattern involves death and rebirth at its core, Miss Miller's hero, Chiwantopel, lives a different fate. Jung writes:

> Chiwantopel, playing the role of the author, is not yet wounded or killed.[45]

The hero in Miss Miller's story doesn't finally descend. From her current state of psychological development, she will not be able to understand the meaning of Chiwantopel's attitude and action.

> He is the bold adventurer who dares to do what Miss Miller obviously shrinks from doing; he offers himself, of his own free will, as a target for the fatal arrow-shot. The fact that this gesture of self-exposure is projected upon a masculine figure is direct proof that the dreamer is quite unconscious of its necessity. ... The animus is not a real man at all; he is a slightly hysterical, infantile hero whose longing to be loved shows through the gaps in his armour. It is in this garb that Miss Miller has dressed the critical decisions of her life, or rather these decisions have not yet got beyond the state of unconscious fantasy and are still not recognized by her conscious mind as her own decisions.[46]

Her problem is that this hero is proud, which means that she is proud. The hero will not allow himself to be killed, which means that she is not going to allow herself to go inside and see what needs to be learned concerning her psychological condition and journey.

Now, Jung steps back to being a bit Freudian:

> The whole of the libido is needed for the battle of life. The dreamer cannot bring herself to this decision, which would tear aside all sentimental attachments to childhood, to father and mother, and yet it must be taken if she wishes to follow the call of her individual destiny.[47]

---

[45] Ibid., par. 462.
[46] Ibid.
[47] Ibid., par. 463.

38

As we have recognized, the whole point of living through a period of transition is to gain access to the superior knowledge in the unconscious regarding how our life can evolve.

The Most Important Words

Jung puts it this way:

> Whoever sets foot in this realm [the unconscious] submits his conscious ego-personality to the *controlling influence of the unconscious*... .[48]

The little statement, "the controlling influence of the unconscious," is typical of early Jung. It is a very important first formulation, but it is an inadequate formulation. Jung will spend the rest of his life expanding on that statement. As a first formulation, it's one we will build on; this initial understanding will be refined throughout his writing during his lifetime and summarized in his final works— which we will consider in detail in the following chapters. Just how does the unconscious affect us? And what do we have to do so it can affect us properly? How does Jung comprehend these questions to provide a broader, deeper grasp of the creative impact of the unconscious on our conscious decisions, on the recognition of our life path, and indeed, on our entire life? He spent his lifetime on these questions.

Jung repeats the early formulation a few paragraphs later:

> The unconscious takes over *the forward-striving function*, the process of transformation in time, and breaks the deadlock. The contents then pouring into consciousness are archetypal representations of what the conscious mind should have experienced if deadlock was to be avoided.[49]

"The controlling influence of the unconscious" and "the forward-striving function" I consider among the most important phrases of *Symbols of Transformation*. We saw the first formulation of this

---

[48] Ibid., par. 508. [emphasis added]
[49] Ibid., par. 617. [emphasis added]

39

concept when Jung talked about "teleology." It is essential to appreciate that Jung set the agenda for the rest of his psychological opus with these statements. And with these statements, Jung has widened our grasp of human motivation, indeed the grasp of our entire life. Something of immense intelligence, something that, so to speak, oversees the creation of our life's meaning, he could empirically show, lies just beyond the easy reach of consciousness.[50] But it *is* there. This aspect of life attesting to the foundational reality that confirms we don't live in a meaningless universe is in each of us. Something is going on that is bigger than we are, of which we are a part. For my tastes, this is Jung writ large. It's why, even though sometimes Jung's prose may leave us scratching our heads, the effort to digest it is amply worth it. Life is no accident, and he knows that. This realization is rapidly becoming an endangered species in our cynical age. In analytical psychology, this fact is Jung's central axis.

Sacrifice

Sadly, and with this more intricate view of the hero, we see further into where and why Miss Miller stumbles.

> Miss Miller's ego is separated by a gulf from the figure of Chiwantopel. ... There will never be any possibility of a meeting or union of conscious and unconscious, the one thing needed to compensate the conscious attitude and create wholeness. ... The situation holds no favorable prognosis for Miss Miller.[51]

In other words, she will not be in a position to understand the Chiwantopel image. What the image represents is a statement about who she is, and this knowledge is in her unconscious. It is trying to

---

[50] This, for Jung, is the *spirit*. Marie-Louise von Franz in *Number and Time,* page 214, has thoughtfully offered us a definition of spirit: "That factor that creates images in the inner field of vision [in other words, creates dreams and fantasies] and organizes [that's the key word here] them into a meaningful order." Why, when we understand a dream or fantasy, is the next image that appears to us a step ahead of the previous one? There is a factor in us purposefully arranging our psychological material toward the fulfillment of our life goals. That is spirit.

[51] *Symbols of Transformation*, par. 614.

communicate information to her, to bring her conscious personality more in line with how the unconscious image is capable of guiding her. In a successful situation, the conscious personality would be able to hear the meaning of that image and make a change. With Miss Miller, it doesn't happen. That is what Jung means by a "meeting or union of conscious and unconscious"—in other words, an understanding on the part of consciousness of the meaning of the image which is generated from within the unconscious. We need these images to reorient us so we can go forward to the fulfillment of our destiny, that destiny coming to us piece by piece in the images we find in the descent into the unconscious.

A tangential discussion follows from the role of the hero. It has to do with sacrifice. Jung observes:

> The instinctive desire, or libido, is given up in order that it may be regained in new form ... .[52]

Miss Miller would have to sacrifice aspects of her understanding of herself. She would have to hear the meaning of her poetry—hear the meaning of the images that emerge from inside. And, in doing so, she would have to discard old views of herself that work against her future. This involves

> a sacrifice ...to the unconscious, which spontaneously attracts energy from the conscious mind because it has strayed too far from its roots ... .[53]

In other words:

> Consciousness gives up its power and possessions in the interests of the unconscious.[54]

Hearing the meaning of her image is giving up power and possession. And that is not always so easy to do.

---

[52] Ibid., par. 671.
[53] Ibid.
[54] Ibid.

The Practical Use of Symbols of Transformation

Here are Jung's concluding remarks about what he would have done in therapy.

> It is hardly to be supposed that Miss Miller, who evidently had not the faintest clue as to the real meaning of her visions—which even Théodore Flournoy, despite his fine feeling for values, could do nothing to explain—would be able to meet the next phase of the process, namely the assimilation of the hero to her conscious personality.[55]

In other words, to hear the meaning of that image.

> In order to do so she would have had to recognize what fate demanded of her, and what was the meaning of the bizarre images that had broken in upon her consciousness. ... The instinctual impulse that was trying to rouse the dreamer ... was opposed by a personal pride that was distinctly out of place,[56]

That would be the arrogance of Chiwantopel.

> and also ... by a correspondingly narrow moral horizon, so that there was nothing to help her understand the spiritual content of the symbols. ... Had I treated Miss Miller I would have had to tell her some of the things of which I have written in this book in order to build up her conscious mind to the point where it could have understood the contents of the collective unconscious.[57]

What's Next?

It's the inner guidance that Jung focuses on in all his psychological efforts. The "forward-striving function," those three little words, Jung studied with meticulous care throughout his life to understand how it works and what it asks of us in order for it to work. His first expression of the function here is a good and, at times, adequate formulation. Sometimes the guidance appears in dreams in a

---

[55] Ibid., par. 683.
[56] Ibid.
[57] Ibid.

straightforward way. But often, there is a lot more to recognize in terms of evoking it and following it, as Jung came to realize and as he set about exploring. To the process and fruits of that exploration, we turn in the following chapters.

MYSTERIUM CONIUNCTIONIS, PART ONE

The next work we'll consider is *Mysterium Coniunctionis*. Jung spent ten years writing the book,[58] while his other volumes took him roughly a few months. Jung considered *Mysterium* his magnum opus, his large or main work. It occupied the last phase of Jung's life. I have chosen to discuss *Mysterium* next because it presents his fundamental insights concerning the nature of psychological healing. The other books we'll examine can be seen growing from his magnum opus.

In the previous chapter, we talked about two types of thinking: directed or linear thinking and symbolic or cluster or imaginative thinking. *Mysterium,* a study of images written from the symbolic point of view, is pure symbolic thinking; it is not linear thinking. The book is a direct view into the working of the unconscious and is uncontaminated by theorizing and intellectual distancing. It is simply a record of inner experience, the kind of experience that emerges when we begin to take the inner life seriously, either out of desperation at a disorienting cul-de-sac in life or out of genuine curiosity for its own sake. I will first present an overview of the book, and then we will look at representative sections to give a sense of how Jung's mind works and how he came to understand psychological growth from the point of view of the unconscious.

Overview

Mysterium focuses on alchemical symbolism. Alchemy, for our purposes, was an enterprise carried on by medieval pre-chemists who chemically worked with materials and thought, in their mind's eye, they were transforming some worthless material into gold, diamonds, or some elixir that would promote world wealth or world peace. They wrote in an imaginative language. They didn't say, "take two grams of sulphur or two grams of salt." They would say, "take two grams of the sun," as the sun was thought to be sulfurous, or "take two

---

[58] Barbara Hannah, *Jung: His Life and Work*, pp. 311, 333; C.G. Jung, *Mysterium Coniunctionis, The Collected Works of C.G. Jung*, vol. 14, p. xiii.

44

grams of the moon," as the moon and salt were linked in the imagination of the alchemists. They expressed in symbolic language what they thought was going on in the material. Jung interpreted their experience of the material, being linked to mythological beings in their mind, as a projection of something going on in themselves. When they imagined they saw a transformation in these mythologically experienced material substances, Jung held that was a projection of a process of transformation in themselves, seen outwardly as a process of transformation in material. His work was to study the alchemical understanding of the transformation of material and to interpret that as a metaphor for the psychological transformation of our inner personality.

Why alchemy? Alchemy lends itself very easily to the psychological transformation process that we are talking about through its metaphoric significance. Alchemy was the last time that the Western non-linear mind, the symbolic mind, operated freely and was unimpeded by the rule of logic prior to the Enlightenment.[59] With the Enlightenment, the writing of the alchemists was dismissed as superstition. In his alchemical studies, Jung didn't fundamentally make use of Egyptian myth because alchemy absorbed Egyptian myth. He didn't refer solely to Greek myth because alchemy absorbed Greek myth. The alchemists thought symbolically with all the mythological traditions of the past. Their work is peppered with images from ancient world culture. In turning the clock back to alchemical writing containing influences from all ancient mythologies, Jung returned to the time when the symbolic mind was still alive. Alchemical imagery is very helpful for understanding the transformation process because it shows the major paradigms of the relation between the ego and the unconscious, which we first met in *Symbols of Transformation*. The alchemists described, in their "pre-scientific" descriptions of material transformations, the same patterns of images Jung discovered inwardly, in persons (and himself) transforming psychologically. The alchemists described the changes they imagined were going on in substances in a way that, as

---

[59] C.G. Jung, "The Philosophical Tree," *Alchemical Studies, The Collected Works of C.G. Jung*, vol. 13, par. 353.

metaphors, could be recognized as symbolizing changes in the journey of personal growth.

Jung also brings in another mythological tradition, related thematically to alchemy, and that is Gnosticism. There are two major thematic paradigms described by the alchemists that Jung recognized as descriptive metaphors for psychological growth. These are: (1) the opposites and their synthesis—for the alchemists, the opposites of conflicting entities or beings imagined in a material substance; for Jung, the opposites of two conflicting emotional states, and (2) the extraction of something, some essence, from within something else—for the alchemists, the extraction of a spiritual essence from concrete, material substance; for Jung, the extraction of meaning from difficult life experiences. The latter thematic paradigm is richly described in the symbolism of Gnosticism. For this paradigm, Jung will turn to Gnosticism as a guiding metaphor that enriches alchemy's vivid portrayal of extraction.

The overall intent of *Mysterium Coniunctionis* is the investigation of alchemical symbolism. In this sense, we will largely examine the central alchemical theme of opposites and their synthesis—with attention to extraction and the Gnostic relevance to it. In the upcoming chapter on *Aion*, we will again examine the theme of extraction, particularly with reference to the last two thousand years of Western history.

After that overview, we begin with Jung's survey of the theme of synthesis and extraction. Then we will explore several sections, in this chapter and the next, dealing with the typical pairs of opposites we are likely to find as we explore our unconscious experience at depth.

The First Sentence

The first sentence of *Mysterium* is a good starting place. "The factors which come together in the coniunctio are conceived as opposites, either confronting one another in enmity or attracting one another in love."[60]

The emotional confusion that we find in our lives when we turn back to ourselves in times of distress is made up of opposites in conflict. When we are in an outer situation in life that has become a problem—a marriage problem, a work problem, depression, despair, you name it—Jung recognized that behind that state is an emotional condition of chaos, which analytic work then begins to explore. When we explore those emotions—in terms of the language in *Symbols of Transformation*, when the hero turns back to the unconscious—what we will often find is opposites in conflict. Note how Jung's grasp of growth has deepened and widened as he dives into the unconscious which guides. At times, in his expanded view, the inner focus meets a pair of opposites that has to be contended with. Those opposites can be either opposites attracting each other or opposites in opposition to each other. Whatever outer problem is presented, in analytic work, we try to find the inner chaos that is part of the experience of the outer problem. We tend to that inner chaos until we see what opposites are in conflict. If we can take responsibility for those opposites and own them as parts of ourselves, as opposed to simply blaming the outside world for the problems in our life, we prepare the way for their synthesis and our growth. This is a fundamental starting point for Jungian work in depth.

Jung starts off with that very basic idea, and then he gives example after example of those opposites. For example, the opposites may symbolize themselves in dreams as two animals in conflict, as two people fighting, as two forces each trying to destroy the other, as two substances in a toxic connection. The pairs of opposites may vary almost infinitely. Often the relation between the two is negative, but

---

[60] *Mysterium Coniunctionis*, par. 1.

not always. The connection between the two can be amorous, erotic, or pleasurable, but often with something unsatisfactory about it.

I will look at some of the alchemical texts Jung examines in order to give examples of various alchemical instances of conflict, of how the conflict looks, and how the resolution of the conflict may unfold.

The Solar Table

Figure 3

This example follows from an alchemical picture published alongside Jung's commentary. (See figure 3.) These figures are goddesses. Jung writes:

> The goddesses represent the four seasons of the sun in the circle of the Zodiac (Aries, Cancer, Libra, Capricorn) and at the same time the four degrees of heating, as well as the four elements "combined" around the circular table. The synthesis of the elements is effected by means of the

48

circular movement in time (*circulatio, rota* [the alchemists used the Latin]) of the sun through the houses of the Zodiac.[61]

These words describe a picture that, for the alchemists, signified an alchemical process. They don't make sense to us because the alchemists intentionally wrote in a very cryptic manner. Through this picture, they are saying that the transformation of a worthless material, lead for example, or transformation of a worthless chaos into gold, is a process whereby four elements in the original, worthless material gather around a table, a common space, and are brought into a unity by virtue of the sun traversing the heavens.

In the mind of a medieval alchemist, this picture, a picture from a medieval manuscript, shows four different chemical elements symbolized here by the four sun-goddesses. They are juxtaposed to each other, i.e., in conflict. From a picture like this, the alchemist knew to heat a first material, such as lead or some worthless substance, in the right way to bring these four goddesses to the table. As the sun, then, goes through the course of the heavens, these four figures at the table are to be brought into unity. When that unity is produced, gold, or some highly valuable endpoint, is produced.

In Jung's understanding, this is what happens when we turn back to ourselves. We look at all the different parts of ourselves that are not in harmony—where we are in conflict with ourselves. We face them. We bring them into awareness, seeking a single awareness. This is represented in the picture as sitting at the table. If we maintain awareness of the conflicting parts, they will harmonize into the unity symbolized by the table. That end point, now going back to *Symbols of Transformation*, is the guidance of the unconscious, the future-creating spirit as noted previously. But in order to find that guidance, the labor of attending to the opposites is necessary to bring forth the single awareness of who we are as a solid, not divided, personality.

The unity of the personality is the knowledge of who we are in essence, which can lead us forward to a genuine life. That genuineness is constructed, so to speak, out of the conflicting

---

[61] Ibid., par. 5.

elements as our attention to the parts of ourselves activates an inner process to unify them.

Here is the puzzle. The book is called *Mysterium Coniunctionis—mysterious* union. How does it happen that when we take responsibility for the conflicting ingredients of our own psyche, synthesis happens? We don't know why. We don't know how. We only know that synthesis happens and that it is a mystery. We don't produce the synthesis. We produce the preconditions, namely, by getting all our pieces around the table—in other words, admitting all our tendencies.

That's the basic idea of alchemical synthesis. The book comes back to this basic idea again and again and again. It presents all sorts of variations on the figures that are in conflict, the typical images used in the dreams to symbolize those conflicts, the typical images expressed in dreams to symbolize the resolution of that conflict. This is what Jung studied in the alchemical texts: all the variety of ways the process of the synthesis of opposites is symbolized and all the variety of ways that it is resolved. That is what we are going to look at. Once we have grasped the basic idea, we are less likely to get lost in the details. If we can keep the basic theme of his intent in this book in mind, it is a lot easier to stay on track.

Ostanes Caught in Heimarmene

I will cite the next text verbatim from Jung's writing. It's an alchemical text Jung is simply quoting for us from a medieval manuscript that he collected. A few brief observations are in order before I do. Ostanes is the name of the alchemist. Heimarmene means the compulsion of the stars. Heimarmene means we are controlled by external forces represented by the astrological constellations. Here, however, the control conveys something negative. We are controlled by a compulsion radiating from the stars, and we can't free ourselves from that. We could roughly say "unwelcome fated influences" that are issuing in a destructive way from the arrangement of the heavens. So Ostanes is caught. He feels caught by a disagreeable fate. These fateful powers that have caught him are emanating from the stars and have vexed him.

> "Ostanes said, Save me, O my God, for I stand between two exalted brilliancies known for their wickedness, and between two dim lights; each of them has reached me and I know not how to save myself from them."

Ostanes feels controlled by polarities that are descending from heaven and are manipulating his life. He doesn't feel free. He has, in psychological parlance, projected his opposites onto the heavens and feels his problem is coming from there.

> "And it was said to me, Go up to Agathodaimon the Great … "

Agathodaimon means the good serpent, the good demon.

> "and ask aid of him, and know that there is in thee somewhat of his nature, which will never be corrupted … ."

The opposites are the powers that he is caught in. Now the beginning of the solution to his problem is this ascent to the good demon.

> "And when I ascended into the air he said to me, Take the child of the bird which is mixed with redness and spread for the gold its bed which comes forth from the glass, and place it in its vessel whence it has no power to come out except when thou desirest, and leave it until its moistness has departed."[62]

Jung explains what that means.

> The quaternio [the four] in this case evidently consists of the two *malefici* [two malevolent influences], Mars and Saturn (Mars is the ruler of Aries, Saturn of Capricorn); the two "dim lights" would then be feminine ones, the moon (ruler of Cancer) and Venus (ruler of Libra). The opposites between which Ostanes stands are thus masculine / feminine on the one hand and good / evil on the other. [They are the opposites, the conflicting forces.] The way he speaks of the four

---

[62] Ibid., par. 5. The entire passage is from par. 5.

luminaries—he does not know how to save himself from them—suggests that he is subject to Heimarmene, the compulsion of the stars; that is to a transconscious factor beyond the reach of the human will.

In other words, Ostanes is possessed by powers that are beyond his willpower to cope with.

Apart from this compulsion, the injurious effect of the four planets is due to the fact that each of them exerts its specific influence on man and makes him a diversity of persons, whereas he should be one.

So we are progressing from conflict to unity. That is the basic model.

It is presumably Hermes[63] who points out to Ostanes that something incorruptible is in his nature which he shares with the Agathodaimon, something divine, obviously the germ of unity.

That potential for wholeness is there. What the process of facing the opposites does is activates the potential to come into life. This is simply the way we are built. That's part of the mystery.

This germ is the gold [now we get different words for the end state, these are not really important for our beginning purposes, but they are worth mentioning], the *aurum philosophorum* [the gold of the philosophers, the alchemists called themselves philosophers; they distinguished between the alchemists' gold, which is a spiritual gold, versus the crude gold, which is material wealth], the bird of Hermes or the son of the bird, who is the same as the *filius philosophorum* [the son of the philosophers, another term for the end state, for what is produced out of the alchemical process]. He must be enclosed in the *vas Hermeticum* [the alchemical vessel] and heated until the "moistness" [his contamination with the chaos of the unconscious state] that still clings to him has departed, i.e., the *humidum radicale* (radical moisture), the prima materia [another word for the beginning state], which is the original chaos and the sea (the unconscious). Some kind of coming to consciousness seems indicated.

---

[63] Hermes, in brief, is a *mythological* personification of the entire alchemical process from beginning to end—and also the transformative potency that makes that happen.

In the alchemist's mind, the process must be cooked—literally cooked in a flask in the alchemist's laboratory. In the psychological interpretation, cooking would refer to tension and suffering that has to be endured. Emotional growth involves heated emotions, in other words. Through enduring these emotions, we begin to have an intimation of where we are headed in ourselves, and through the heated feelings involved in facing ourselves, we give that intimation a chance to become fully realized.

> We know that the synthesis of the four was one of the main preoccupations of alchemy, as was, though to a lesser degree, the synthesis of the several (metals, for instance). Thus in the same text Hermes says to the Sun: ...

> "I cause to come out to thee the spirits of thy brethren [the planets], O Sun, and I make them for thee a crown the like of which was never seen;"

Here is another image of the redeemed condition: the crown. Circular images are what we can expect as the conflicting elements come into a unity.

> "and I cause thee and them to be within me, and I will make thy kingdom vigorous."

The production of the resolved condition brings back the vigor that was lost when the conflict demoralized us.

> This refers to the synthesis of the planets or metals with the sun, to form a crown which will be "within" Hermes. The crown signifies the kingly totality; it stands for unity and is not subject to Heimarmene.[64]

The end condition gives one the strength not to be controlled and flipped back and forth between these opposing forces that were once felt to be so devastating. The "forces" that once controlled us are now felt as essential ingredients in a larger whole of a stronger and more genuine personality. Their compulsiveness has dissolved into the larger whole. They are felt as personality attributes that add to the

---

[64] *Mysterium Coniunctionis*, par. 6. The preceding quotes are all from par. 6.

quality of life and not as compulsions that seem determined to destroy it.

Something "new" gets started as the opposites are synthesized, to put it another way. The crown is an image of that something "new." In Jung's words, it's the Self born in an individual—*our genuine person created out of difficulties*. It is born not in spite of difficulties but out of difficulties.

The Self may be a new term for some readers. This concept is certainly one of Jung's major contributions to psychology. Our understanding of his concept will develop as we proceed, but a few introductory comments are in order. Jung holds that we are born who we are capable of becoming. In other words, the potential of our identity, the potential for who and what we are, is inborn.[65] But it is lost in childhood. Adapting to reality, the demands of family life, even with the best of parents, and pressures from school, for example, often do little to help us realize this identity. In fact, these experiences in life almost universally try to alienate us from our birthright. One of the ways we reconnect with our genuine selfhood is by carrying our opposites consciously when they are activated, as in the case of the alchemical recipe we are considering. When the opposition gives way to synthesis, the "unity" that is restored is a piece of the real us that has been hidden in an unconscious state. Each process of conflict and synthesis returns a bit of our original personhood to us, our original Self. The Self, then, is what we lose throughout early life, but we have a chance to recover in time through devoted psychological work that reaches the depths reconstituting our central core as opposites yield up their hidden unity.

The first paradigm described in *Mysterium* is separation and synthesis or union, for which we've seen two examples. I've noted there is another paradigm that occupies Jung's attention, and that is the paradigm of extraction. For this paradigm, Jung turns to Gnosticism.

---

[65] Jung often refers to the phrase *a priori*, i.e. before experience. "The Self is *a priori*" is the way this is expressed in Jungian psychology.

Gnosticism

Gnosticism is a name given to a set of religious groups prevalent at the birth of Christianity. But it's also clear that Gnosticism existed before Christianity, as Gnosticism is known in early Judaism. What we now call the Christian Church is simply the coalescing, among many different theologies around the life of Christ, of one point of view into official theology. Gnosticism is the name given to one grouping of those competing interpretations, and these sects were later declared heresy by what we call the Church. The Gnostics have different understandings of divinity, but they all share a couple of basic tenets. The main tenet is that when God created the world, God got trapped in the world. There are many different varieties of how that happened within the various Gnostic sects. But they all had the supposition that there were little sparks of God embedded in the world. There was a little spark of God in each of us. Gnostic religion concerns how the faithful should live so that at death or at the return of the redeemer, the piece of God in them goes back to the main God.

In the Gnostic mind, it is not individuals who need redemption; it is God. At the creation of the world, part of God is lost in the world, and God has to be, so to speak, put back together again. The divine gets trapped in the material world and must be remade. The text we are going to look at as an example is from Manichaeism. Manichaeism is one type of Gnosticism.

In the Manichean tradition, a divine Messenger is sent to the lower world to rescue the trapped divine Light. The Messenger seduces the dark powers holding the Light and forces them "to release their Light either by sweating it out of them or by ejaculation."[66]

Figure 4

Edward Edinger explicates this comfortably as he writes in his commentary on *Mysterium Coniunctionis*. "One aspect of the analytic process, in which one opens up the unconscious and exposes the ego to the contents of the unconscious, makes visible various desires that had long been dormant." Linking this activity within the analytic journey with the Gnostic metaphor of extraction, he interprets: "Consciousness sends a messenger ... to entertain ... forbidden desires ... . A kind of sweat box is generated that can lead to the extraction of the light stuff imprisoned in the unconscious complexes."[67] (See figure 4.)

---

[66] Edward Edinger, *The Mysterium Lectures*, p. 50.
[67] This and the previous quote are from *Mysterium Lectures*, pp. 51f.

The Gnostic idea is that the God trapped in matter must be released. The psychological interpretation suggests that when we live our difficult emotions, our difficult desires, we can ask the right kind of questions like: "Why am I in this situation?" and "Why do I feel this way?" and "Why is this state of mind plaguing me?" and "What emotions are driving me and could they be here to teach me something?" As we commit to such an inquiry, meaning is extracted out of the experience. In other words, there is some meaningful advice for us *within the experience of difficult states of mind.* That meaningful advice is the positive influence of the unconscious embedded in our difficulty. Where the end point of the union of opposites is understood as the image that synthesizes our contradictions into a more harmonious condition of personal, even social, harmony and integrity, the goal of the Gnostic metaphor is the recognition of deep insight into who we are, how we are to live, the steps we can take to become that person of significance. That is the metaphoric understanding of the "light" of the Gnostics, psychologically understood. By holding in our experience and with an open heart the difficult emotional moments of our life, the meaning of these moments in the form of valuable insight becomes available to us, generally through a dream or an overwhelming intuition.

I will cite an example of extraction from within an alchemical text. This is to alert us to how this theme looks when it appears in alchemy. To make this recipe a bit easier to digest, I am not quoting Jung's direct commentary. Rather I will present Edinger's discussion on the text, which is a bit easier to follow as we become more familiar with the mind of the alchemists.

The Senior Text

For the text in question in *Mysterium Coniunctionis*,[68] I will quote from Edinger's *Mysterium Lectures'* summary for the sake of brevity and clarity.

Senior is the Western name of an influential Arabic alchemist.[69] Alchemy is said to have initially appeared in Egypt, a derivative of embalming symbolism. Then it was picked up by the Muslims, and from the Muslims, it was introduced into Europe. Many of our early sources of alchemy have been passed on from the Arabic culture. Alchemy came to the West partly through the Crusades and partly through Spain when the Arabs shot up through northern Africa into Spain and France. This next text was originally an Arabic text that was translated into Latin. Edinger summarizes the text for us.

A child is to be born.[70]

The *filius* is the end point, for example, the guidance from the unconscious that we are trying to find. This brings us back to the inner guidance of the unconscious we met first in *Symbols of Transformation* in terms of "the controlling influence of the unconscious" and "the forward-striving function." Note, here, however, the conditions for the appearance of inner guidance must be created by considerable effort.

A house must be built for its birth, and this house is the alchemical vessel. The text says that this house is actually a tomb inhabited by either witches or serpents, or both, who feed off the blood of sacrificed black goats.

---

[68] *Mysterium Coniunctionis*, pars. 77–83
[69] "Ibn Umayl," Wikipedia, last updated August 12, 2022, https://en.wikipedia.org/wiki/Ibn_Umayl. He was an early Muslim alchemist who lived from c. 900 to c. 960 AD. In Arabic his name was Muḥammad ibn Umayl al-Tamīmī.
[70] Remember, this an alchemist speaking so the child is the *filius* that's to be born out of the alchemical retort, also called the alchemical vessel.

58

These infernal creatures fight with each other, copulate with each other, and conceive and give birth all in an unholy composite, a mess.

The unholy composite mess is a metaphor that equates to the mess of life that we've been talking about.

> The text says they remain in this state, in the tomb-house, for forty days. ... At the end of it, the male serpents cast their semen on the white marble ... . Ravens gather this semen and carry it to the tops of the mountains. The ravens then become white and they multiply.[71]

Note the Gnostic allusion. The same idea in Gnosticism is expressed in the text as a substance *extracted* by a sort of seduction and expulsion, the casting and gathering of the semen.

Now Edinger interprets:

> This describes a process going on in the alchemical retort; it's easy to forget that because the imagery gets so picturesque. The child to be born out of this tomb-vessel is the lapis, [also called] the son of the philosophers. But the contents in the vessel are black, evil, reptilian: serpents, witches and blood of black goats. It's a real witches' brew. But that vivid feature is also what makes it so valuable for us psychologically, because it corresponds to a certain aspect of unconscious stuff when first encountered—it's very noxious. And it is crucial that this noxious stuff be contained for the forty-day period.

We have to begin owning that the emotional poison and chaos is in us, that it is coming from a part of ourselves. The challenge is not to let it spill out into the world in fits of blaming or in moments of acting out our distress on others.

> If it seeps out into the environment, the result is all sorts of evil, vicious, paranoid activity. ...

We blame somebody else for what we have inside ourselves.

---

[71] Edinger's summary of the text is from *Mysterium Lectures*, p. 79.

Edinger continues:

> If it's subjected to the forty days of containment (corresponding to Christ's forty-day temptation in the wilderness), then it is transformed.

> That transformation is described by the interesting image of the serpent's semen being cast onto the white marble. ... The creative power is *extracted* from the dark contents—from the reptilian level of the psyche—and transformed to the upper realms, to the ravens. ... The effect on the birds who gather it up is to transform them from black birds to white birds.[72]

The preceding text/recipe gives, in the form of images, the idea of extraction out of experience, of our containing the chaos of a problematic experience until the message of the experience gives itself up. This "incubation" of our onslaughts of lust, or rage, of frustration, or heartache allows the creative aspect of the unconscious to begin communicating, in image form, the meaning of what we are going through. This "creative power" of the unconscious is yet another formulation of "the forward striving function" of the unconscious. In *Symbols of Transformation*, consciousness simply dips into the inner world and receives the guidance. With the alchemists, interpretated psychologically, opposites are carried until there is the emergence of an emotional synthesis, the return of the original Self, guiding us forward. The Gnostic view shows that the effort the ego has to make is to face life's difficult experiences and extract the wisdom for our life that is meant to be communicated to us by the upheaval we are going through. We sit with our dreams in these ordeals and watch the meaning of our onslaught appear in the form of intelligent images from within. This is the extraction. Then we can take steps to address that meaning and to live it in time and space.

It is the therapist's job to help analysands hold their experience and to be capable of their own distress until their own inner voice leads them forward. For the therapist, often this means simply being

---

[72] Edinger's interpretation is from *Mysterium Lectures*, pp. 79f. [emphasis added]

present as the analysand deals with themself. This means helping the analysand ask the right questions. At other times this might mean encouragement: "Don't give up, I have been through something similar myself; hang in there." The analyst has to be able to speak *from their own experiences*. These betwixt-and-between times can be terribly demoralizing. Remember the title of Jung's book: for Jung, the moments of transformation are a mystery. They just happen. But we have to create the precondition for the mystery's happening by our inner attentiveness, our understanding of how the difficulty is symbolized in dreams, by fully feeling the period of difficult stagnation. The psyche knows its own—and our unique—direction. What we have to do is prepare the way to hear our own advice.

A Look Ahead

Mysterium has first introduced, in sections I and II, the general alchemical and Gnostic paradigms—the theme of opposites and their synthesis and the theme of extraction. Now the work considers typical personifications of pairs of opposites that we find in alchemical literature. Section III concerns opposites of the sun and the moon (and their related images of sulphur and salt as well as the lion and the dog). Section IV focuses on the pair of the king and the queen. Section V pertains to the polarity of Adam and Eve. The last section VI deals with the theme of union under the title "The Conjunction." In this chapter we will survey section III. The following chapter in this book will consider sections IV through VI of *Mysterium*.

Section III, Sol (sun) and Luna (moon)

The first typical representation of the initial opposites we'll consider is Sol and Luna, in other words, the sun and moon. The sun is bright in contrast to the moon, which is dim. The sun is hot and blinding, whereas the moon is gentle and subtle. These opposites, sun and moon, could stand for just about any pair of opposites in us where there is a contrast that has to do with bright and dim, or masculine and feminine, or yang and yin, if you prefer. The sun and the moon can be images our dreams use to symbolize the polarity of a given

61

pair of opposites having to do with bright and dark emotional realities. The practical value of knowing this symbolism is that when we see these images in dreams, we can recognize that we are dealing with opposites and the need for synthesis.

Jung observes, in a tangential comment worth noting, that Sol can represent one pole of the opposites, or it can also represent the Self. That difference is outside our scope here. But it is not too hard to imagine there can be different possibilities of meaning for a single image. When we realize the job of the ego is to hear the intimations of who we really are, i.e., of the Self—and to reflect them to the world around us—Sol's further meaning isn't so puzzling. This real person in us has to come into harmony with the way we actually live. Sometimes the sun can represent one of the opposites, sometimes it can represent the goal—at least the bright clarity of seeing the goal. The meaning of the sun will then depend on the context. Edinger puts it this way:

> So the sun as the symbol of consciousness represents both the ego and the Self. The reason for that double representation is that the Self cannot come into conscious, effective existence except through the agency of an ego. Needless to say it can come into plenty of effective existence without an ego but it cannot come into consciously effective existence without the agency of an ego. This is why it is unavoidable that the symbolism of Sol, as the principle of consciousness, represents both the ego and the Self.[73]

Sulphur, a major image in the alchemical text to be explored, is the chemical equivalent of Sol as one of the opposites. It can be seen as representing the masculine principle of burning desire. Sulphur can also represent soul. Jung puts it this way:

> Sulphur represents the active substance of the sun or, in psychological language, *the motive factor in consciousness*: on the one hand the will, which can best be regarded as a dynamism subordinated to consciousness, and on the other hand compulsion, an involuntary motivation or impulse ranging from mere interest to possession proper. The unconscious dynamism would correspond to sulphur, for

---

[73] Ibid., p. 94.

compulsion is the great mystery of human life. It is the thwarting of our conscious will and our reason by an inflammable element within us, appearing now as a consuming fire and now as life-giving warmth.[74]

On the one hand, we can control our will. However, where there is lust, or passion, or desire, or a marriage triangle, or there is great resentment, all of that would also be symbolized by sulphur, namely, where we are burning. It doesn't mean we are necessarily happy to be burning, but burning we are, nevertheless.

The problem with burning is that it functions outside of what we generally wish for our life. So the burning is not necessarily felt as a benevolence, but we are possessed by it anyway. We are stuck with the fact that we can't get rid of it, but if we live out the possession concretely in the wrong way, we can destroy everything we have ever worked for, everything that is dear to us.

Sulphur is often the beginning of the alchemical process in that it is what leads us to these worldly situations that we have to resolve. Sulphur would represent crude desire. The lion's hunting prowess and voracious roar are perfect descriptors of the power of sulphur. There is also a refined sulphur in alchemy, which represents when the crude desire has been transformed into a higher level of cultural living—soulful desire that is gentler and more generative, hence the reference to soul.[75] However, generally, we get nailed by sulphur in its crude form—desire in its compulsive and overpowering aspect. And we have to do something about it if we want to digest and humanize its energy without being damaged psychologically or literally.

That's the sun, generally speaking, as one of a pair of opposites. I focused on sulphur because it is so closely tied to sun symbolism and because sulphur appears below in the alchemical text. It is also worth a reminder that the animal form of sulphur is the lion. That doesn't

---

[74] *Mysterium Coniunctionis*, par. 151.
[75] The transformation from crude to refined sulphur is a leitmotif of the "Moisten this dry earth" text below.

seem too hard to imagine, as I noted, in the hunting fervor and roaring voice of human desire.

The other opposite is typically symbolized by the moon. The moon would personify the receptive, the feminine, or if you prefer, the yin, the hidden, the quiet, the secretive, the feeling, as opposed to the lethal and devouring light and desire of the sun. The sun is loud; the moon is quiet. Those qualities of the moon regenerate in darkness.

Where the chemical equivalent of the sun is sulphur, the chemical equivalent of the moon is salt. Whereas we have discussed sulphur as desire, we will see that salt has two meanings: bitterness and wisdom. Although salt does not appear in the recipe to follow, the salt image, in general, is so important I want to discuss it.

Jung writes:

> Apart from its lunar wetness and its terrestrial nature, the most outstanding properties of salt are bitterness and wisdom. ...

Jung is just citing how the alchemists describe salt as representing or embodying either bitterness or wisdom.

> Tears, sorrow, and disappointment are bitter, but wisdom is the comforter in all psychic suffering. Indeed, bitterness and wisdom form a pair of alternatives: where there is bitterness wisdom is lacking, and where wisdom is there can be no bitterness.[76]

Sulphur leads us into experiences. It is the itching desire that leads us into events. When the hoped-for result of the event does not work out the way we wanted for any one of a variety of reasons, salt, so to speak, is the result. We get bitter. We wanted something, and we didn't get it. In other words, desire can lead to bitterness when we are frustrated in obtaining what we want. If we reflect on the disappointment in the way we've been discussing, and if we can extract the meaning of the experience—going back to our discussion

---

[76] The two-part quote is from *Mysterium Coniunctionis*, par. 330.

of extraction—we become wise. That is how salt can represent either bitterness or wisdom.

It is important that our desire moves us into life, and it is important that we seek what we want. If we *don't* get what we want, then we do well to turn back to ourselves and ask, "Why? What is the meaning of this frustration?" Until we find the meaning of our frustrated sulphur, our life urge will have produced salt as bitterness. When we do understand the meaning of the apparent failure, another piece of ourselves will come to us, as the salt of bitterness becomes the salt of wisdom.

Salt, as the chemical form of the moon, will not appear in the following recipe, but the dog, as the animal form of the moon, will. The animal that is typically attached to the moon symbolism is the dog. The dog represents the dark side of the moon. The dog as a howling animal symbolizes the gnawing, depressing, biting thoughts we have during the process of transformation. The light side of the moon would be the positive, gentle dimension of receptiveness and relationship. The dark side would be the discomforting thoughts that plague us. We don't like that part of the process because it is so unpleasant. But it is essential to be able to feel what we *don't* want, to feel where we are unhappy, sad, unsatisfied, so that we can move toward what we *do* want. Both sides of what the moon symbolizes have to be reckoned with in this process. Particularly in the United States, we are taught to be what is "great," bright, all positive (solar), are we not? That leaves no room for the difficulties (canine lunar) of growth to our deepest Self.

If sulphur and the moon can unite, we can transform solar burning into something of long-term and creative value for ourselves and those around us ... if the synthesis can be dealt with after the opposites are accepted and the mystery of their transformation given sufficient time and space in our lives.

That was a quick tour of the sun and moon, just to give you a taste of how Jung's presentations of the material work. We hear many examples of lions and dogs, sulphur and salt, sun and moon. Jung compiles images to broaden out the images that appear in our dreams when we are in the throes of dealing with the opposites. Knowing what to expect and knowing the background of the images that can appear in the dreams help us to stay oriented to the healing occurring in us as we confront ourselves.

With this rudimentary grasp of the symbolism of the sun and moon, I will next discuss a text Jung cites from the medieval alchemical literature. I find it a beautiful text. It is presented verbatim from an alchemical manuscript, possibly dating back to the 17th century. I've extracted Jung's basic comments on each symbolic point. I'll be giving direct quotes from Jung's commentary.

Moisten This Dry Earth

Here's the text, an alchemical recipe:

(1) "If thou knowest how to moisten this dry earth with its own water, thou wilt loosen the pores of the earth, (2) and this thief from outside will be cast out with the workers of wickedness, (3) and the water, by an admixture of the true Sulphur, will be cleansed from the leprous filth and from the superfluous dropsical fluid, (4) and thou wilt have in thy power the fount of the Knight of Treviso,[77] whose waters are rightfully dedicated to the maiden Diana."

Diana is Artemis in Greece, a huntress. Her animal is the dog.

(5) "Worthless is this thief, armed with the malignity of arsenic, from whom the winged youth fleeth, shuddering. (6) And though the central water is his bride, yet dare he not display his most ardent love towards her, because of the snares of the thief, whose machinations are in truth unavoidable. (7) Here may Diana be propitious to thee, who knoweth how to tame wild beasts, (8) and whose twin doves will temper the malignity of the air with their wings, (9) so that the youth easily entereth in through the pores, and instantly shaketh the foundations of the earth, and raises up a dark cloud. (10) But thou wilt lead the waters up even to the brightness of the moon, (11) and the darkness that was upon the face

---

[77] Bernardus Trevisanus, see *Mysterium Coniunctionis*, par. 74.

of the deep shall be scattered by the spirit moving over the waters. Thus by God's command shall the Light appear."[78]

I've numbered the sentences to assist in making the commentary easier to follow.

(1) "If thou knowest how to moisten this dry earth with its own water, thou wilt loosen the pores of the earth,"[79]

Here's Jung on that sentence:

(1) If you will contemplate your lack of ... inner aliveness ... and impregnate it with the interest born of alarm at your inner death, then something can take shape in you, for your inner emptiness conceals just as great a fullness if only you will allow it to penetrate into you.[80]

That is putting into other words what we've been saying. The point expressed is to focus on the darkness that we are dealing with in a given experience. Don't run from it; let it be as we have to give our attention to it to turn misery into meaning.

(2) "and this thief from outside will be cast out with the workers of wickedness,"[81]
Jung comments:

(2) Something like an evil spirit has stopped up ... the fountain of your soul. The enemy is your own crude sulphur, [your problematic passion] which burns you with the hellish fire of desirousness or *concupiscentia* [unbridled desire]. ... You no longer even want to be fruitful, as it would be for God's sake but unfortunately not for your own.[82]

That last sentence is, of course, said ironically. The text points out how we get tied to the outcome of our efforts, its rewards and personal recognition, instead of seeing the efforts as in the service of

---

[78] Ibid., par. 186.
[79] Ibid., par. 189.
[80] Ibid., par. 190.
[81] Ibid.
[82] Ibid., par. 191.

a higher principle. That is because of our greed. Put at its most basic, that is the unconscious condition we tend not to work on because we say, "What good is it?", rather than working on it for its own sake and watching what it gives back to us as we find our path to authenticity.

> (3) "and the water, by an admixture of the true Sulphur, will be cleansed from the leprous filth and from the superfluous dropsical fluid," [83]

Jung writes:

> (3) Therefore away with your crude and vulgar desirousness, which childishly and shortsightedly sees only goals within its own narrow horizon.

That's the key thing, "within its own narrow horizon." In other words, "What's in it for me?"

> Admittedly sulphur is a vital spirit ... ;

Desire *is* important, in other words, but

> useful as it is at times, it is an obstacle between you and your goal. The water of your interest is not pure, it is poisoned by the leprosy of desirousness which is the common ill. You too are infected with this collective sickness. ... What is behind all this desirousness? A thirsting for the eternal ... . For desire only burns in order to burn itself out, and in and from this fire arises the true living spirit, which generates life according to its own laws, and is not blinded by the shortsightedness of our intentions or the crude presumption of our superstitious belief in the will. ... [84]

He is not talking about not wanting things in life. What he is driving at is when we want something, and we can't get it; nevertheless, we keep seeking after it with maniacal drivenness, while ignoring all indications to the contrary. That is the crude sulphur. "I will have it,"

---

[83] Ibid.
[84] This and the previous two quotations are from *Mysterium Coniunctionis*, par. 192.

even though things repeatedly and stubbornly are not working out. I manipulate and cajole to get something that, in the long run, will have deleterious effect on me or those around us. To cite a few examples: the higher position in the corporation that saps our strength, the glamorous and sexy relationship that beats down our self-esteem, or the bigger car to make us look important. Even if, by hook or crook, the object is achieved, we are generally left with an emptiness, perhaps even despair. The candy in the candy shop wasn't so sweet after all.

Those words "true living spirit" are *essential*. Desirousness, it is also important to point out, often has the end point of bringing us to the "true living spirit." There is a real guidance for our lives embedded in difficult experiences if we can work with the difficulty and not simply take the difficulty only literally. In our analytic work, we encourage our analysands both to live through the experience and to turn to the unconscious in that process to let the dreams first guide them through the problem, then also to let the dreams, in time, point out the meaning of the experience.

We are, in effect, revisiting the phrase the "true living spirit," Jung's early formulation in *Symbols of Transformation* that the "unconscious takes over the forward-striving function." The discussion of the "true living spirit" in *Mysterium* is a more differentiated formulation of the "forward-striving function" where we first met the definition of spirit. The discussion in this chapter has shown how the ego must often create the preconditions for the emergence of inner guidance from the inner knowledge of our own unique selfhood initially hidden in unconsciousness. I mentioned, when we discussed *Symbols of Transformation*, that Jung's later works return to the early formulation in that work to widen, deepen, and recognize the intricacies of the processes that announce, in the best sense, our destined path in life. The discussion of the "true living spirit" develops his first formulation, as does his consideration of extraction we just explored. In *Symbols of Transformation*, simply a descent into the unconscious was the precondition to uncover the forward-striving function. At times, for our path to the genuine future to be revealed, more is asked of our effort in the form of dedicated scrutiny and reconciliation of opposites.

"The true living spirit" seeks to be realized on its own terms:
> The unconscious demands your interest for its own sake and wants to be accepted for what it is.[85]

Through conscientious psychological effort, which Jung continues to describe, growth can evolve.

> Once the existence of this opposite is accepted, the ego can and should come to terms with its demands.[86] Unless the content given you by the unconscious is acknowledged, its compensatory effect is not only nullified, but actually changes into its opposite, as it then tries to realize itself literally and concretely.[87]

We continue seeking, with increased effort, the understanding which at first eludes us.

> (4) "and thou wilt have in thy power the fount of the Knight of Treviso, whose waters are rightfully dedicated to the maiden Diana."[88]

Jung describes:

> (4) The ever flowing fountain expresses a continual flow of interest toward the unconscious, a kind of constant attention or "religio,"[89] which might also be called devotion. ... If attention is directed to the unconscious, the unconscious will yield up its contents, and these in turn will fructify the conscious like a fountain of living water.[90]

---

[85] Ibid.

[86] By devotedly watching present and future dreams, or by engaging in active imagination, for example. In both cases, Robert Johnson's *Inner Work* is a thoughtful "how to" book, a guide for dreamwork and for active imagination.

[87] *Mysterium Coniunctionis*, par. 192.

[88] Ibid.

[89] "Religio" is one possible etymology of the word religion, and it suggests the original meaning of the word religion has to do with "paying constant attention to."

[90] *Mysterium Coniunctionis*, par. 193.

All of that can happen when we give up compulsively pushing for what it appears, after our best concerted effort, that life will not grant us. When the door to the object of our obsessive desire closes on us, despite all our efforts, and when we begin to try to understand the meaning of our desire for it our life can be nourished with entry into our genuine selfhood.

> (5) "Worthless is this thief, armed with the malignity of arsenic, from whom the winged youth fleeth, shuddering."[91]

Jung again:

> (5) The thief ... personifies a kind of self-robbery. He is not easily shaken off, as it comes from a habit of thinking supported by tradition and milieu alike: anything that cannot be exploited ... is uninteresting—hence the devaluation of the psyche.[92]

We have discussed the raw or low form of sulphur. The other side of raw sulphur, we noted briefly, is the transformed intensity of the compulsive sulphur having reached our consciousness as an ongoing, genuine creative engagement with life, in the way our destiny has wanted to shape us.

> The thief is contrasted with the winged youth, who represents the other aspect, or personifies the "true sulphur," the spirit of inner truth which measures man not by his relation to the mass but by his relation to the mystery of the psyche. ... The shy and delicate youth stands for everything that is winged in the psyche or that would like to sprout wings. But it dies from the poison of organizational thinking and mass statistics; the individual succumbs to the madness that sooner or later overtakes every mass—the death instinct of the lemmings.[93]

A lemming is a small vole-like animal; common belief has it that when one lemming jumps off a cliff, they all do. The winged youth would represent that way of living which is the fulfillment of what

---

[91] Ibid.
[92] *Mysterium Coniunctionis*, par. 194.
[93] Ibid., pars. 196f.

we are really seeking, the realization of our genuine Self: what our real talents are, what a real relationship is, what a real home is, as opposed to following that we are seeking illusory goals of power, prestige, accumulation, and so on. I particularly like the way Marie-Louise von Franz has put it: PPFF (power, prestige, fame, and fortune).[94]

(6) "And though the central water is his bride, yet dare he not display his most ardent love towards her, because of the snares of the thief, whose machinations are in truth unavoidable."[95]

I particularly appreciate Jung's comments here:

(6) The goal of the winged youth is a higher one than the fulfillment of collective ideals. ... [A person's] life is the soil in which his soul can and must develop. He has only the mystery of his living soul to set against the overwhelming might and brutality of collective convictions. ... I can do no more than demonstrate the existence of this image [the winged youth] and its phenomenology. ... If [a person] no longer sees the meaning of his life in its fulfillment, and no longer believes in man's eternal right to this fulfillment, then he has betrayed and lost his soul, substituting for it a madness which only leads to destruction, as our time demonstrates all too clearly.[96]

The fulfillment of our own life's meaning is what that winged youth stands for. What will really be satisfying? What profession will feed our soul? What relationship will fill us? What kind of home will be where life flourishes and love can grow, whether it's a trendy McMansion or a small, cookie-cutter suburban ranch in the middle of nowhere.

The alchemical text continues:

(7) "Here may Diana be propitious to thee, who knoweth how to tame wild beasts,[97]

---

[94] A well-known aphorism of Dr. von Franz's.
[95] *Mysterium Coniunctionis*, par. 197.
[96] Ibid., pars. 198, 201.
[97] Ibid., par. 203.

(8) and whose twin doves will temper the malignity of the air with their wings,"[98]

And Jung's reflections follow:

(7) The darkness which is opposed to the light is the unbridled instinctuality of nature that asserts itself despite all consciousness. (8) The tender pair of doves is an obviously harmless aspect of the same instinctuality. ... Together they represent the attack, first from the one side and then from the other, of a dualistic being on the more restricted consciousness of man. The purpose or result of this assault is the widening of consciousness. ... The one-after-another is a bearable prelude to the deeper knowledge of the side-by-side, for this is an incomparably more difficult problem.[99]

The instincts are what shuttle us back and forth. The dove would be the message to come to us like we saw, the wisdom born out of the conflict that we are dealing with as we stay true to it. Jung says "harmless" because that's the beneficial aspect of the experience if we know how to get the wisdom out of being tossed back and forth between the opposites.

The text continues:

(9) "so that the youth easily entereth in through the pores, and instantly shaketh the foundations of the earth, and raises up a dark cloud."[100]

Jung's response:

(9) It is the prefiguration and anticipation of a future condition.[101]

That is the condition of living a meaningful life from a knowledge of genuine selfhood that is solid and enduring.

The text continues:

---

[98] Ibid., par. 204.
[99] Ibid. pars. 204f.
[100] Ibid., par. 206.
[101] Ibid., par. 208.

(10) "But thou wilt lead the waters up even to the brightness of the moon,"[102]

Jung's words are to the point:

(10) As we have seen, water here has the meaning of "fructifying interest" ... .[103]

The text describes the shift from darkness to inspired living:

(11) "and the darkness that was upon the face of the deep shall be scattered by the spirit moving over the waters. Thus by God's command shall the Light appear."[104]

Jung concludes:

(11) The eye that hitherto saw only the darkness and danger of evil turns towards the circle of the moon, where the eternal realm of the immortals begins, and the gloomy deep can be left to its own devices, for the spirit now moves it from within, convulses and transforms it.[105]

The spirit, the inner guidance that holds the knowledge and trajectory of how our life is to develop, is, as noted, a later articulation of that first phrasing, "the unconscious takes over the forward-striving function."

---

[102] Ibid., par. 209.
[103] Ibid.
[104] Ibid., par. 210.
[105] Ibid., par. 211.

74

MYSTERIUM CONIUNCTIONIS, PART TWO

In the previous chapter, we canvassed Jung's general presentation of what he means by "the opposites" in the first sentence of *Mysterium*. We also touched on the Gnostic theme of extraction. We discussed the solar table followed by Ostanes caught in Heimarmene. The first pair of opposites that Jung singled out as very typical representations of the opposites, the sun and the moon, next occupied our attention. In this chapter, we will look at two more typical pairs of opposites that Jung presents, the king and the queen, as well as the polarity of Adam and Eve. We will end this chapter with his reflections on the nature of alchemical and psychological union.

The King and the Queen

The discussion of kings and queens is a very important one. The king and queen theme, expressed in images of literal kings and queens, does not show up frequently in dreams of people from the United States because we are a nation that was founded in rebellion to kingship. What royalty psychologically represents for us is more likely to appear in dreams of the president or the principal of a school, for instance—some generally recognized authority figure. However, since the political reality of king and queen is so common worldwide, and because king and queen images appear frequently in the literature of alchemy, I'll be talking about the psychology of those figures in terms the alchemists do, namely as a king and a queen.

> The further we go back in history the more evident does the king's divinity become. ... The king was the magical source of welfare and prosperity for the entire organic community of man, animal, and plant; from him flowed the life and prosperity of his subjects, the increase of the herds, and the fertility of the land. This signification of kingship was not invented *a posteriori*;[106] it is a psychic *a priori*[107] which reaches far

---

[106] After experience.
[107] Before experience—as noted in the previous chapter.

back into prehistory and comes very close to being a natural revelation of the psychic structure.[108]

Let's put that in our own words.

Jung surveys the history of kingship beginning with Egypt. Egyptian society was arranged around a king. All the rituals of that society were based on maintaining a relationship to the king—and on keeping the king potent. In that early society's mind, if the crops failed or there was social disorder, it was because the king wasn't doing his job. So they killed him. Being a king was a risky business. (See figure 5.)

Figure 5

Then they would install a new king with a new set of rituals to make sure the new king had potency and power. Where did he get his power? From God.

Earliest societies were based around God, who had relationship not to the individuals in society but to the king. The individuals in the society maintained their relationship to God through their relationship to the king. The king's power coming from God is what made social harmony possible, what made crops fertile, and what made animals fecund.

There is, then, a hierarchy of God ruling king and king ruling society. Jung feels that pattern is an externalization of the fundamental structure of the personality. Taken as a metaphor, God would represent the Self, the creative center of the personality.

---

[108] C.G. Jung, *Mysterium Coniunctionis*, *The Collected Works of C.G. Jung*, vol. 14, par. 349.

In the previous chapter, we saw the Self guiding the personality to the realization of the person we are to be in our lifetime. I suggested this Self guiding occurs as we work on recovering our essence and manifests when we make an effort to create the conditions for its emergence. By seeking the synthesis of our conflicting opposites (the alchemical model) and by seeking to extract lessons of our real identity from complicated desires and life situations (the Gnostic model), we find our inner guidance to full selfhood.

The Self influences us through images that represent and communicate the state of affairs of our essence. A similar dynamic is, on a grand scale, evident in historical kingship. The historical pattern of God's influence on society is parallel, metaphorically speaking, to the Self's influence on the inspirations that form us.

Now I add another consideration. The Self's influence, within the same process that is returning our real core to ourselves, is, at the same time, affecting the reshaping of our personal values. As we recover our genuine identity, our values change in the process of our coming closer to our *a priori* essence. Significant inner figures representing our value system can be observed evolving in their dream portrayal as our life values develop appropriate to the particular phase of our life beckoning us and the particular challenges our destiny may wish fulfilled.

This is true on a social scale as well. The authority figures we find in dreams reflecting the development of values and outlooks can be seen in images of kingship on both a social level or a personal level. As stated above, in the US, the image is more likely to be a president, a political figure, a school principal—some respected authority.

The nature of the Self, the nature of our essence, changes over time throughout the course of our life. The state of the Self in a child is different than the state of the Self in a young mother, is different than the state of Self in an empty nester, and is different than the state of the Self in a person facing death. There is a development within the Self throughout life. Jung writes:

> The king, like every archetype, is not just a static image; he signifies a dynamic process ... .[109]

The king (or some version of his authority) as the portrait of the functioning value system, which in the optimum state is a reflection of our essence, must change because the essence of the personality changes in the different phases of our life. Or putting it very simply, our values change throughout life, and they are meant to change.

This is as true for the individual as it is for society. Individuals go through periods of change in which values need to be reevaluated and transformed, just as a society must reexamine and reevaluate what it generally finds valuable as it faces new challenges and fresh demands.

Another way to say this is that the king has to go through a periodic process of death and rebirth.

An essential theme in alchemy is the transformation of the king. In the recipes we'll be looking at, the medieval mind thought that through their "chemical" work, they were taking an old king in the worthless material and turning that old king into a healthy king. When that new healthy king is born, the worthless material will turn into gold or some version of the precious end point—or so they believed. By looking at the symbolism of the king and his transformation in alchemy, we learn a lot about what the psyche goes through as it shifts its values. For Jung, this is important because he doesn't feel that it's only the past that causes present problems. His feeling is that an inadequate value system in the present, one that has become out of date as life evolves, can be a potent cause of psychological problems. Those inadequate value systems need to be transformed. In order to transform them, sometimes we have to go back to the past to accrue what we lost. The past isn't causing our problems; the present is causing them because our values are not "up to date." The king is an enormously cogent image for Jung's fundamental standpoint. What is at issue in psychological growth is a recognition and transformation of values, that is, the system of what

---

[109] Ibid., par. 356.

is important to us. The king image is really a process, a process whereby value systems are transformed so that they represent the inner state of the Self that is, itself, a dynamic evolving process.

We'll explore two alchemical texts that show the king's transformation to give a sense of how Jung worked with the king theme. By examining these texts, we can learn from Jung how we can understand the growth process that is expressed in metaphor in the alchemical texts. Both of the texts I'll discuss are medieval.

This section on the king and the queen in *Mysterium* consists of text after text where Jung cites a text in which there are royal figures, and then he interprets it. If we know one text and have a feeling about how Jung works with it, then we have a background that makes digging into subsequent text more accessible. It is so easy to get lost in the details, but if we remember that what he is discussing are different examples of the king's and queen's transformation, it's easier to grasp Jung's writing.

The Allegory of Merlin[110]

> The allegory tells us of a certain king who made ready for battle. As he was about to mount his horse he wished for a drink of water. A servant asked him what water he would like, and the king answered: "I demand the water which is closest to my heart and which likes me above all things." When the servant brought it the king drank so much that "all his limbs were filled and all his veins inflated, and he himself became discoloured."[111]

All of this shows how the king, i.e., the prevailing value system, is sick—it is based in greed. Sound familiar?

> His solders urged him to mount his horse, but he said he could not: "I am heavy and my head hurts me, and it seems to me as though all my limbs were falling apart." He demanded to be placed in a heated chamber where he could sweat the water out. But when, after a while,

---

[110] 14th or 15th century (The Alchemy Website, "The Allegory of Merlin," http://www.levity.com/alchemy/merlin.html).
[111] *Mysterium Coniunctionis*, par. 357.

they opened the chamber he lay there as if dead. ... The Egyptian physicians ... tore the king into little pieces, ground them to powder, mixed them with their "moistening" medicines, and put the king back in his heated chamber as before. After some time they fetched him out again half-dead. ... They ... washed him with sweet water ...mixed him with new substances. Then they put him back in the chamber as before. When they took him out this time he was really dead. But the physicians said: "We have killed him that he may become better and stronger in this world after his resurrection on the day of judgment."[112]

This theme of killing the king, or the king's drowning or otherwise meeting his demise, is a very common theme in alchemy and certainly in dreams. The imagery shows the psyche's tendency to destroy value systems that are no longer working.

The king's relatives, however, considered them mountebanks, took their medicines away from them, and drove them out of the kingdom. ... The Alexandrian physicians took the body, ground it to powder a second time, washed it well until nothing of the previous medicines remained, and dried it. Then they took one part of sal ammoniac [rock salt] and two parts of Alexandrian nitre [saltpetre], mixed them with the pulverized corpse, made it into a paste with a little linseed oil, and place it in a crucible-shaped chamber. ... Then they heaped fire upon it and melted it. ... Whereupon the king rose up from death and cried in a loud voice: "Where are my enemies? I shall kill them all if they do not submit to me."[113]

Here's a summary of Jung's interpretation.

The king personifies a hypertrophy of the ego which calls for compensation.[114]

Hypertrophy of the ego would refer to a person who is inflated and puffed up—a big shot. In this recipe, the king represents the value systems of a big shot: Mr. Big Stuff. The values of someone who is overbearing, obnoxious, self-centered, and pushy are what this king would stand for. In modern language, this would be the value system

---

[112] Ibid.
[113] Ibid.
[114] Ibid., par. 365.

of a narcissist. In an individual case in the therapy situation, we are working with someone who is dominated by the egotistical value system. We would try to help them see how they are out of balance with themselves. This can be very difficult since such distortions are very much the style of the time, in fact, the style of *our* time.

The recipe deals with a king, which would mean, at the most prosaic and practical level, it is basically dealing with a standard of masculine behavior. Of course, we have both standards of masculine behavior and feminine behavior in us—this recipe can be seen slanted to the masculine side. In the case of a woman, if the king belonged to a woman's psyche, it would represent the masculine dominant values controlling certain aspects of her life.

Typically, the king represents masculine values, and the queen represents feminine values. We're talking about the king so much because that's the image that shows up in alchemy. Traditionally, for a woman, it would be just the opposite. It wouldn't be the king; it would be the queen who goes through a death and rebirth. Typically, a woman would be dreaming of queens, but now both sexes are dreaming of kings and queens. A man *could* dream of a queen when it is a question of his values in the area of relationship, or the yin side of life, and a king when it is his values in terms of outer, perhaps yang, societal or professional involvement. A woman *could* dream of a king when it is a matter of her outer, perhaps yang, societal and professional involvement and a queen when it is a question of her values in the area of relationship or the yin side of life. Please note I used the word *could*. It seems to me that this is one of the most misunderstood aspects of Jungian psychology, that these mythological patterns are to be forced on our experience. Particularly after his correspondence with Wolfgang Pauli, Jung rephrased his position to talk about the *probability* that a certain form would mean such-and-such.[115] There is an equal probability that the form will *not*

---

[115] Wolfgang Pauli was one of the key scientists involved in the formulation of the Copenhagen interpretation of quantum mechanics in 1927. His 1951 challenging Jung to understand the archetype as the *probability* of psychic events Jung felt extremely insightful. This position expanded the archetype from being conceptualized as the possibility of a

mean such-and-such. How many arguments have started with statements like, "Well, Jung said that this means that," and so on? His final realization, again in his correspondence with Pauli, is that we are dealing with probabilities of occurrence. The art of working with this material consists in knowing the general patterns as probabilities, comparing our provisional grasp of the structure of the psyche with the reality of the person in front of us, and using our *feeling* to find our way through the development of individual experience and growth. To wit: my supervising analyst in Zürich, C.A. Meier, *never* probed what the concept told about an experience. He asked what the experience tells us about the concept. The concept is always malleable.

This common assumption seems to be reliably true. Whether in a male or female, when we see in dreams that the inner authority figure is under assault, we know that the person's value system is no longer workable and is in need of transformation. We need to have the agility of mind and the background of imagistic history to, in dialogue with the other, unravel just what that transformation is to consist of.

I'll continue with the king's arrogance. The image that often appears in the dreams of people who are living out this kind of big shot psychology is that they are very thirsty; their drinking is compulsive. Even when they are saturated, they still are thirsty. I recall a billboard I saw in the Dallas airport during a layover, which read: "You can never have too much." That message is from a world that is driven by thirst, but a thirst that is never quenched. The thirst may be for money, power, possessions, status, you name it, but they are never enough. As a metaphor, I'd say the thirst images in dreams indicate that the flow of life is no longer satisfying. Why? Because the values around such greed don't direct the eternally consuming person to the part of life that would be satisfying. So they are driven to bigger this and bigger that—the thirst they are accruing is driven by acquisition until they burst. That bursting could show up as depression, an

---

definable pattern to being conceptualized as the probability of a pattern within a wide range of possibilities. Carl Jung and Wolfgang Pauli, *Atom and Archetype*, especially pages 69f.

outburst of emotions, perhaps a suicide attempt, or a car accident. Sometimes it shows up inwardly as misery, or sometimes it shows up outwardly as a catastrophe. We often find that when we examine an external catastrophe, it has been preceded by an internal catastrophe. The external difficulty is an externalization of the inner.

Jung reminds us that it is a moral issue:

> He is about to commit an act of violence—a sure sign of his morally defective state.[116]

The value system can no longer guide the individual in moral action. The more such a person has, the more they want. Jung refers to this as concupiscence, unbridled desire, which opens the individual to an assault of all possible accumulated thirsts and hungers from the unconscious:

> His thirst is due to his boundless concupiscence and egotism. But when he drinks he is overwhelmed by the unconscious.[117]

We then note in the recipe of two attempts to heal the king. One set of physicians is Egyptian, and the other is Alexandrian. The former fails to rejuvenate the king, and the latter succeeds. Jung sums up the difference.

> The difference between the Egyptian and the Alexandrian physicians seems to be that the former moistened the corpse but the latter dried it .... The technical error of the Egyptians, therefore, was that they did not separate the conscious from the unconscious sufficiently, whereas the Alexandrians avoided this mistake.[118]

That would mean that a reductive analysis is necessary at this point. Reductive analysis in therapy means examining current attitudes which are out of tune with life and reality for their origins in past experiences. The challenge is to recognize the errors, see where they

---

[116] *Mysterium Coniunctionis*, par 365.
[117] Ibid.
[118] Ibid.

came from, and make the effort to change them. As a simple example, we might say that the reason someone has a need for a McMansion is that the person has inferiority feelings which come from the past.

We have to begin reflecting on "what is the genuine way to live my life?" In my example, we must recognize the source of inferiority feelings and how we might go about avoiding them by always trying to look important (versus *being* important). We have to understand those feelings and recognize how avoiding them has created life goals that are empty. Then we can begin reflecting on how to live so that life is genuinely satisfying.

> Certainly there is little trace of this in our somewhat crude parable. Also, the transformation of the king seems to betoken only the primitive renewal of his life-force, for the king's first remark after his resuscitation shows that his bellicosity is undiminished.[119]

The king starts out pugnacious, and he ends up pugnacious. There is really not a deep transformation. The king, the representative of the value system, would be the value system of somebody who is arrogant and pushy. And that never changes. The person just ends up better at being pugnacious. There was no real transformation; the person just apparently learned to cope better.

This is just the first recipe we'll look at from the section on the king and the queen. As there really is no transformation at all, we'll look at another that goes deeper, and then compare the two. Jung continues:

> In the later texts, however, the end-product is never just a strengthening, rejuvenation or renewal of the initial state but a transformation into a higher nature.[120]

In the "Allegory," there is no real confrontation of opposites or struggle with extraction. The end point of the text is correspondingly unremarkable.

---

[119] Ibid., par. 367.
[120] Ibid.

Ripley's "Cantilena"

The title of this next text is Ripley's "Cantilena." It is attributed to Sir George Ripley (c. 1415–1490), who was an English Augustinian canon, author, and alchemist.[121]

> "There was a certaine Barren King by birth,"

Right off the bat, there is a barren king. The value system is not creating any fertility in life.

> "Composed of the Purest, Noblest Earth, | By nature Sanguine and Devoute, yet hee | Sadly bewailed his Authorite."

So the king here is shown as old, impotent, and sad. The value system is not working.

> "Wherefore am I a King, and Head of all"

Just compare that with the last recipe; there is doubt here, not battle-ready hubris.

> "Those Men and Things that be Corporeall? | I have no issue, yet I'le not deny | Tis Mee both Heaven and Earth are Rulèd by."[122]

"No issue" would mean no children. That value system is not able to continue generating new understandings that life might require. Nothing new can come out of it. The king's customary ruling capacity is here shown as very lame.

Nothing healing can flow from the existing value system; there is no flow of life, and all is stagnant:

---

[121] "George Ripley (alchemist)," Wikipedia, last modified July 9, 2022, https://en.wikipedia.org/wiki/George_Ripley_(alchemist).

[122] *Mysterium Coniunctionis*, par. 370. verses one through five.

"Alas, my Nature is Restricted so | No Tincture from my Body yet can flow. | It therefore is Infoecund: neither can | It ought avail, in Generating Man."[123]

From the following lines, we are shocked to find who the king is:

"My Mother in a Sphaere gave birth to mee, | That I might contemplate Rotunditie; | And be more Pure of kind than other things, | By Right of Dignity the Peer of Kings. | Yet to my Griefe I know, unless I feed | On the Specifics I so sorely need | I cannot Generate: to my Amaze | The End draws near for me, Ancient of Daies."[124]

There are a couple of themes to notice. One is the rotundity. It is representative of wholeness—and in the most complete way, we can understand what our life needs to make it meaningful. That is the circle business.

The other image is that the king himself needs to feed. He has specific needs. Here is where the ego must put energy into this process for it to succeed. Once the transformation process of a value system starts, we have to give it regular attention through dreamwork.

The "Ancient of Days" is something Jung makes a great deal of because it is the way Yahweh is described in the Hebrew Bible, in Daniel 7 : 9.[125]

I beheld till the thrones were cast down, and the Ancient of Days did sit, whose garment was white as snow, and the hair of his head like the pure wool: his throne was like the fiery flame, and his wheels as burning fire.[126]

Ultimately what we are working on in the king image is an understanding of what God is in a given time period. The transformation of the God-image is the deepest layer of this

---

[123] Ibid., par. 372, verse seven.
[124] Ibid., pars. 373f. verses nine and ten.
[125] King James Version.
[126] *Mysterium Coniunctionis*, par. 374.

alchemical journey. Because those values represented by the king are ultimately based on how we understand God.

This text originated in the fifteenth century, yet it foreshadows our spiritual dilemma in the third millennium. We are living through the collapse of all religious certainty, the demise of many values Christianity has held dear, and the release of such anti-social and down-right criminal behavior as to nearly numb the mind—in all levels of social living, at all levels of so-called political authority.

"And therefore, that I may be Borne agen, | I'le Humbled be into my Mother's Breast, | Dissolve to my First Matter, and there rest."[127]

That is an image of disorientation. The values are dissolved and, so to speak, go back to the unconscious, meaning that the conscious personality no longer knows what is important—and what is left is trust in this inner development within the unconscious to begin reforming another value system. The way this is experienced is that we are living in a period of despair and disorientation. Whether we are talking about the loss of religious values in the individual or in the body politic, at this point in the disorientation, all we know is that something needs to be created—and all we can experience is nothingness. The art of the work involves enduring that dark night of the soul, until the unconscious becomes creative and begins to show the way.

A meaningful quote from Jung is worth considering:

Dissolution is the prerequisite for redemption.[128]

Dissolution is the despair, the loss of orientation, the confusion. And this is what we must go through to get to the new condition of finding the meaningful way forward in life. This is not a pleasant thought, but it is a true thought. This is why analysis is so unpopular. If you can become a new person with seven new habits, why bother with this stuff? All those seven new habits do is keep you better at your

---

[127] Ibid., par. 380, verse twelve.
[128] Ibid., par. 381.

old value system. When the self-help movement is about picking yourself up and getting yourself going again, all that does is to keep the old values working. It helps you stay afloat with the old values. The only way to have a fundamental shift is to be dissolved, which is miserable. And that's why we fight so hard against it. On the other hand, once we have been through this process one time, the next time is not as scary. The second or third or fourth time around, it is not as difficult to get through. We begin to learn that the night precedes the dawn and that the dawn does indeed follow night.

Jung writes of the king's return to his mother's breast for rebirth:

> The king must transform himself into the prima materia in the body of his mother and return to the dark initial state which the alchemists called the "chaos."[129]

Everything we learned in *Symbols of Transformation* concerning incest applies here. Here the opposites are expressed in terms of incest. The text reflects an image of incest but not incest in the regressive sense, rather in the progressive sense of returning to the unconscious to find the inner guidance that it holds for us in these difficult times. The opposites are the ego and the unconscious, and they intermingle.

> "Twas wonderful to see with what a Grace | This Naturall Union made at one Imbrace | Did looke; and by a Bond both Sexes knit, | Like to a Hille and Aire surrounding it."[130]

The embrace of two, the knitting of the sexes, is pure incest, but in the sense of one delving into the other – of one delving into the "otherness" of the maternal unconscious which births.

> "The Mother unto her Chast Chamber goes, | Where in a Bed of Honour she bestows | Her weary'd selfe, 'twixt Sheets as white as Snow | And there makes Signes of her approaching Woe.| Ranke Poison issuing from the Dying Man | Made her pure Orient face look foule and wan: | Hence she commands all Strangers to be gone, | Seals upp her Chamber doore,

---

[129] Ibid.
[130] Ibid., par. 387, verse fourteen.

and lyes Alone. | Meanwhile she of the Peacocks Flesh did Eate (See figure 6.) | And Dranke the Greene-Lyons Blood with that fine Meate, | Which Mercurie, bearing the Dart of Passion, | Brought in a Golden Cupp of Babilon.[131]

Her Skin in divers Colours did appeare, | Now Black, then Greene, anon 'twas Red and Cleare."[132]

Several points stand out here:

The peacock is a very frequent image in dreams. Or the same theme may be expressed as a sunrise with the brilliance of the different colors of dawn. Or a rainbow.

The king has disappeared. The story turns to the mother. That theme of the king's disappearance signals the loss of orientation I just mentioned.

Figure 6

Notice also that it is an incestuous union. As touched on, the incest theme is one place where Jung could not agree with Freud, namely that all dreams of incest meant some type of incest with the parent. The incest image shows up very frequently when it is a question of the king falling back into the unconscious for a renewal, and that

---

[131] Ibid., par. 387, verses fifteen to seventeen.
[132] Ibid., verse nineteen, par. 430.

process of renewal shows up as incest. This gives us another angle to understand incest imagery. It's about a *union* of the old value system with the generative capacity of the unconscious to reorient life.

Here are some interpretive comments:

> Psychologically this would refer to the intense internal direction of the libido during a major psychic gestation.[133]

> The peacock is an allusion to the *cauda pavonis* (peacock's tail) [a term the alchemists used frequently]. Immediately before the *albedo* or *rubedo* "all colours" appear, as if the peacock were spreading his shimmering fan.[134]

The alchemists were describing a physical change in the material, "the iridescent skin that often forms on the surface of molten metal." But Jung took the alchemist's imagery as a metaphor for the psychological change inside.

> The basis for this phenomenon may be the iridescent skin that often forms on the surface of molten metal (e.g., lead). ... They [the colors] all unite in the *albedo* ... . Eating the peacock's flesh is therefore equivalent to integrating the many colours (or, psychologically, the contradictory feeling values) into a single colour, white.[135]

The text is talking about the colors on a metal. Jung sees that as relevant to an aspect of the transformation process and to all the difficult emotions we have to go through in order to fulfil the process of growth and healing. Even if the ego is disempowered from its ability to change our situation and we are disoriented while waiting for our dreams to put us back together, we still have the important job of feeling everything that is going on during this process. The change is not just a mental one but a change of our entire personality. In the alchemical language, that multi-color eventually, in the mind of the alchemist, will turn into a white color—to white hot. As a metaphor for the psychological process, many colors would stand for

---

[133] Edward Edinger, *The Mysterium Lectures*, p. 88.
[134] *Mysterium Coniunctionis*, par. 388.
[135] Ibid.

going through all the emotions that attack us until clarity emerges out of the confusion. That is the white. All the emotions have to be endured to get to the genuine clarity that is not just mental, but which embraces and expresses the totality of our personality.

> The lion expresses the passionate emotionality that precedes the recognition of unconscious contents.[136]

Insight is generally preceded by being on fire with emotions, often bestial emotions.

> The animal form emphasizes that the king is overpowered or overlaid by his animal side and consequently expresses himself only in animal reactions which are nothing but emotions. Emotionality in the sense of uncontrollable affects is essential bestial.[137]

A little further on, in the same spirit, Jung writes:

> The blood of the green lion drunk by the queen is handed to her in a "golden cup of Babylon." This refers to the "great whore" in Rev. 17 : 1ff., "that sitteth upon many waters, with whom the kings of the earth have committed fornication, and the inhabitants of the earth have been made drunk with the wine of her fornication . . . having a golden cup in her hand full of abominations and filthiness of her fornication."[138]

In the Book of Revelation, the whore of Babylon is presented as holding the disgusting sins of the world. But the most important psychological point is that her filthy sins are contained in a *golden* cup she holds. Isn't that interesting? As the Bible presents it, the revolting lowest sin is contained in, held by, the golden cup, a representation of the highest value. Such a description applies to this phase of the emotions in the transformation process. The emotions are often humiliating, denigrating, abhorrent, appalling, repugnant, overpowering—which, though seeming anywhere from uncomfortable to downright immoral to outrageous in the heart of

---

136 Ibid., par. 404.
137 Ibid., par. 405
138 Ibid., par. 414; cf. Edward Edinger, *Archetype of the Apocalypse*, p. 33.

any decent person, are of the highest value—because they contain the seeds of new growth.

The text continues:

> "Thrice Fifty Nights she lay in Grevious Plight, | As many Daies in Mourning sate upright. | The King Revivèd was in Thirty more, | His Birth was Fragrant as the Prim-Rose Flower."[139]

> "Her time being come, the Child Conceiv'd before | Issues re-borne out of her Wombe once more; | And thereupon resumes a Kingly State, | Possessing fully Heaven's Propitious Fate. | The Mother's Bed which erstwhile was a Square | Is shortly made Obicular; | And everywhere the Cover, likewise Round | With Luna's Lustre brightly did abound."[140]

There's the rebirth of the value system.

Jung understands the sweet smell as the fragrance of the Holy Spirit. This shift from death to rebirth of the value system is essentially a *miracle*. This is, I've mentioned, why the book is called *Mysterious Union*. We don't know how that happens.[141]

In Ecclesiastical allegory and in the lives of Saints a sweet smell is one of the manifestations of the Holy Ghost. ... Although they [the alchemists] regarded the art as a charisma, a gift of the Holy Spirit, or of *Sapientia Dei,* it was still man's work and even though a divine miracle was the decisive factor, the mysterious filius was still concocted artificially in a retort.[142]

---

[139] Ibid., par. 431, verse twenty.
[140] Ibid., par. 438, verses twenty-six to twenty-seven.
[141] In the *Dream Analysis: Notes of the Seminar* Jung discussed his analytic work with a man in a sexless marriage. In his account of this man's analysis, Jung reported that one day the man and his wife suddenly resumed physical intimacy. Jung was asked how that happened. He said he didn't know: "I don't know how. It is left to the grace of God, but I can tell you it was very alive. It worked itself out." p. 549. Incidentally, Jung used the word "grace" 21 times in *Mysterium Coniunctionis.*
[142] *Mysterium Coniunctionis*, pars. 432, 443.

Transformation is a balance between human effort and grace. What is needed to evoke the positive, guiding unconscious dynamism? We have to face the opposites; we have to let ourselves be dissolved; we have to endure shattering and often reprehensible emotions; we have to live through the despair to be in the place where the new thing can come in. That comes as grace, but without our effort, grace would not have occurred. Jung is sensitively attuned to this balance between effort and grace.

"The Dark Clouds being Dispers'd, so sate she there,"[143]

The despair is lifting.

"And woven to a Network in her haire | Were Planets, Times, and Signes, the while the King | With his Glad Eyes was her Beleagering."[144]

She was feeding the king.

Here's Jung's commentary:

These melting processes all express a relativization of the dominants of consciousness prevailing in a given age. For those who identify with the dominants or are absolutely dependent on them the melting process appears as a hostile, destructive attack which should be resisted with all one's powers. Others, for whom the dominants no longer mean what they purport to be, see the melting as a longed-for regeneration and enrichment of a system of ideas that has lost its vitality and freshness and is already obsolete.[145]

A value system has been reborn, and that is much of what Jungian work is about. The alchemical text attests to the reality that inner work, working on the transformation of our own values, soon extends out to the values of the time. The two exist, touching each other. Clarifying what is important to us often leads to the recognition that we have been identified with values that the larger body politic espouses, but which we have to separate from. In doing so, we add a

---

[143] Ibid., par. 453, verse thirty-five.
[144] Ibid.
[145] Ibid., par. 455.

tiny drop to the change process that is also trying to occur within the general point of view.

"Thus He of all Triumphant Kings is Chiefe, | Of Bodies sicke the only Grand Reliefe: | Such a Reformist of Defects, that hee | Is worshippe'd both by King and Commonalty.| To Princes, Priests he yields an Ornament, | The Sicke and Needy Sort he doth content: | What man is there this Potion will not bless, | As banishes all thought of Neediness.[146]

Compare that with the "Allegory of Merlin" that we previously discussed. In this text of Ripley's "Cantilena," there has been a fundamental shift in the king who guides with restraint and justice for everyone and not just himself. The other king in the "Allegory of Merlin" was just getting better at being bellicose."

Jung sums up:

If neurotic symptoms appear, then the attitude of consciousness, its ruling idea [i.e., the king], is contradicted, and in the unconscious there is a stirring up of those archetypes that were the most suppressed by the conscious attitude. The therapist then has no other course than to confront the ego with its adversary and thus initiate the melting and recasting process. The confrontation is expressed, in the alchemical myth of the king, as the collision of the masculine, spiritual father-world ruled over by King Sol with the feminine, chthonic mother-world ... or by the chaos. ...The illegitimate aspect of this relationship appears as incest ... which ... results in the pregnancy of the mother [mother being the unconscious]. ... If the ego does not interfere with its irritating rationality, the opposites, just because they are in conflict, will gradually draw together ... . In the end this must lead to some kind of union, even though the union consists at first in an open conflict, and often remains for so a long time. It is a struggle that cannot be abolished by rational means. ... The only certain thing is that both parties will be changed, but what the product of the union will be it is impossible to imagine.[147]

Jung's summation is the creative aspect of the unconscious, leading our lives on their destined trajectory and path. That is the spirit at

---

[146] Ibid., par. 459, verses thirty-six to thirty-seven.
[147] Ibid., pars. 505f., 514.

work: here, royalty, representative of our fundamental values, comes closer to the truth.

Adam and Eve

The next image we will examine is Adam and Eve. We might ask ourselves, "why are these the images Jung talks about?" The reason is that these two figures are one of the ways the alchemists personified the opposites. Jung has gone to alchemical literature and examined the most frequent personifications of the process of opposition and synthesis. We've seen sun and moon, lion and dog, sulphur and salt, then king and queen, and now Adam and Eve.

There is something unique about Adam and Eve, and we'll pick up with that. This is Jung:

> Adam is the transformative substance, the "old Adam" who is to renew himself.[148]

Whereas it was the king who was renewed in the previous section, now it is the figure of Adam who is being renewed.

The biblical text behind this reference to Adam is I Cor. 15 : 22

> "For as in Adam we all die, even so in Christ shall all be made alive." I Cor. 15 : 22 [149]

There is some theology behind that. In the Church Father's view, there was Adam who began the Judeo-Christian story. And then Christ was a second Adam. Just the word "Adam" in the Christian tradition can carry with it the sense of two Adams. The first Adam was thought to be primeval; natural; whole, but by virtue of not being developed—wholeness in a natural state. The second Adam, Christ as the second Adam, is an Adam that has been perfected in Christ. The wholeness in the first Adam, which is natural, becomes a

---

[148] Ibid., par. 550.
[149] *Mysterium Lectures*, p. 256.

95

perfected wholeness in Christ, who is the second Adam. This is all in the mind of the Church Fathers—and in the mind of alchemists.

Jung now interprets these religious or mythological conceptualizations. The Self has two states, and this corresponds to the two Adams. There is a first state of the Self and then a second state of the Self. The first state is the state of childhood wholeness. We are, in potential, what we can become. The goal of analytic work is to realize what we have been made to be in potential—and then to develop and live that potential and have that be the basis on which we live our life.

What does the first and second Adam have to do with individuality? Jung observes:

> That the consciousness of ... individuality should coincide exactly with the reactivation of an archaic god-image is ... a very frequent occurrence which, in my view, corresponds to an unconscious law.[150]

He reached this conclusion simply by observing in patient after patient how, when the person began to feel grounded in themselves, when they began to feel that their life was no accident, when they began to feel that there was a reason for them to be on earth, when they began to feel that this reason was addressed to them, when they began to feel that there was a plan for their life to be fulfilled, they dreamed of images of God (often archaic) advising them, supporting them, guiding them. In other words, genuine personhood, real selfhood, has to do with the discovery that slumbering in the unconscious is the pattern of our life waiting for us to realize it, to bring into time and space the unique individuality we are to develop and the unique contributions that we are to bring into life. This individuality is *not* a state of isolated aloofness, though periods of intense introversion may be necessary in certain periods of our lives to rekindle it—through processes like we have been delineating in paradigms drawn from alchemy and Gnosticism. Quite the opposite,

---

[150] C.G. Jung, "The Relations between the Ego and the Unconscious," *Two Essays on Analytical Psychology, The Collected Works of C.G. Jung*, vol. 7, par. 248.

this individuality (*in* = not, *dividuus* = divided) is a condition of the person which is not divided into episodes of self-sabotage, hypocritical proclamations, and spurious utterings. A single, whole person is making their way in life with forethought and awareness of consequence and integrity. We've seen that this source and inner center Jung calls the Self.

We have seen two of the ways the Self comes into consciousness in the themes of the synthesis of opposites and the extraction of spirit from the, at times, awfulness of life. Again, recall how far Jung has come from *Symbols of Transformation* where the unconscious was simply helpful when one turned back to it. That early and limited formulation of what he later called the "true living spirit" of the unconscious is valid; it is a foundation for the more exacting analysis of what goes on in the birth of individuality that he labored to express for the rest of his life through the books we are exploring.

To the alchemists, just the term "Adam" meant transformation from one state to another because there is a first Adam and there is a second Adam. We could say the first state is an unconscious feeling of completion, and the second state is wholeness constructed with effort, in the way we've been discussing, through a journey into the realization of what we have been given to be and do. Coming up we will see a third state, which we will discuss in terms of the three stages of the coniunctio, and that state has to do with synchronicity.

This is how Jung puts it:

> We must now turn to the question of why it was that Adam should have been selected as a symbol for the prima materia [the first substance worked on in the alchemical vessel; as we just talked about it as a metaphor that would be the conflicted state of mind] or transformative substance. This was probably due, in the first place, to the fact that he was made out of clay ... a piece of the original chaos, of the *massa confusa* [the confused mass], not yet differentiated but capable of differentiation ... [The chaos refers] to the original state of hostility

between the elements, the disorder which the artifex [the alchemist] gradually reduced to order by his operations.[151]

A side note: in some alchemical recipes, rather than just finding Adam, they had to collect him. Adam is often associated with the number four. For example, in one text it is said that: *God collected the dust from which Adam was made from the four corners of the earth.* The initial state sometimes has to be found by effort that looks at things completely in all four directions.[152]

A text with a similar theme is cited by Jung:

> The Pentateuch says, regarding the creation of the first being, that his body was composed of four things, which thereafter were transmitted by heredity: the warm, the cold, the moist, and the dry. He was in fact composed of earth and water, a body and a soul. Dryness came to him from the earth, moisture from the water, heat from the spirit, and cold from the soul.[153]

The same idea is expressed that Adam is made up of four parts, and he has to be constructed into a whole. Psychologically this has to do with *totally* looking at all parts of ourselves and with taking full account of ourselves.

Summing up the general discussion of Adam: there is a primitive beginning with an intentionality leading to an end; in other words, the presence of the unconscious Self, often in a storm of affect, that leads to a conscious realization of the Self individually lived in time and space.

An alchemical recipe with Adam as its main imagery follows. I'll present the recipe, then summarize Jung's interpretation.

---

[151] *Mysterium Coniunctionis*, par. 552.
[152] Ibid.
[153] Ibid.

98

Adam Kadmon

For (1) Noah must wash me in the deepest sea, with pain and toil, that my blackness may depart; I must lie here (2) in the deserts among many serpents, and there is none to pity me; I must be (3) fixed to this black cross, and must be cleansed therefrom with wretchedness and vinegar and made (4) white, that the inwards of my head may be like the sun or Marez [earth], and my heart may shine like a carbuncle, and (5) the old Adam come forth again from me. O! Adam Kadmon, how beautiful art thou! And adorned with the rikmah [many-colored garment] of the King of the World![154]

Here's Jung's commentary and Edinger's summary as a concise interpretation of the text. Again, I've numbered the text and commentary to facilitate our digesting the texts:

(1) It is evident that the speaker is the feminine personification of the prima materia in the *nigredo* state. [The prima materia is the beginning material in the alchemical vessel. The *nigredo* is the first dark state.]... She is "desire:" ... . [That would be the first Adam, the primitive desirousness that starts this process of transformation in some form of desire, either positive or negative, love or resentment, lust or hate.] [She] contains in herself the first Adam, like the mother her child, and at the same time awaits the second Adam, i.e., Adam before the Fall, the perfect Original Man [in the Christian framework that would be Christ].[155]

The feminine personification of the prima materia is the experience of confusion, the emotional feeling of being lost in the black darkness. What has to come out of that confusion, the recipe alludes, is the awareness of the first Adam, an awareness that we are beset by an emotional experience that we need to take seriously and begin to transform.

Adam Kadmon [that's the term that is used] is the image of the Anthropos [the Anthropos would be the image of the completed, fulfilled human being] as it manifests itself in the Kabbalah. He's thought of as the first emanation of the En Sof [the original creative stuff of the

---

[154] Ibid., par. 591.
[155] Ibid., par 592.

universe] and he's also thought of as the totality of the Sefirotic Tree. …
The Kabbalistic idea is that the original creative power—the En Sof
which signifies infinity … emanates; it shines forth out of its potential.
And what it emanates is Adam Kadmon … . According to some versions,
Adam Kadmon then may further emanate the whole Sefirotic tree; or in
other versions the Sephirotic Tree itself can be considered as the body
of Adam Kadmon.[156] (See figure 7.)

Some commentary is necessary to
unpack that. In the Jewish mystical
tradition, the Kabbalah, the creative
power of God is called the En Sof. That
creative power emanates into the world
in the form of the figure called Adam
Kadmon. Adam Kadmon is the
embodiment on the earth of the creative
power. In the mystical tradition, Adam
Kadmon would equate to the second
Adam—Adam comes forth again. It is
said, Edinger notes, that from Adam
Kadmon, a tree emerges. Those different
circles in the illustration depict different
aspects of his divine power. He manifests
the glory of God in many different ways.
The manifestations of the one creative
principle in the form of Adam Kadmon
or the second Adam show up as these
different nodes of a tree.

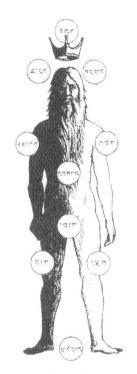

Figure 7

The point of all this is that in the tradition
of the Kabbalah, there is both a first and
a second Adam. In the Christian
tradition, the second Adam would be parallel with Christ; for the
Kabbalah and the Jewish mystics, the second Adam is Adam Kadmon
as a reflection of God's creative energy.

---

[156] *Mysterium Lectures*, pp. 250, 39f.

2) Then, in the second point, come the serpents that, here, have to do with, as we've seen, the emotions that could sidetrack the process because they are too strong. In this instance, being bitten by the serpents represents being bitten by, upset by, distracted by, the negative, sabotaging emotions—the unholy composite mess of the previous chapter.

3) In the next part of the text, the prima materia is being fixed to a cross. Since the cross has four segments, the analogy to the four functions becomes evident. All four functions have to be involved in understanding what we are going through.

4) The white appears. Remember the whiteness? It's the same whiteness, i.e., the emergence of clarity. The previous text emphasized the colors and integrating them. Here, the emphasis is on not being sidetracked by the poison of negativity—by the poison of panic. Such states of mind may encourage us to push our experience away or to go out and act it out in a destructive way.

Edinger sets the stage for Jung's comment:

> (5) So we see that the old Adam is immediately followed by Adam Kadmon, the Anthropos who is called "the King of the World." ... So that the old Adam and Adam Kadmon are merged with each other ... ."[157]

Now Jung:

> Now it is significant that the "old Adam" is mentioned at the very moment when the perfect ... Adam, the shining Primordial man, is obviously meant. ... A change for the better does *not* bring a conversion of darkness into light and of evil into good, but, at most, is a compromise in which the better slightly exceeds the worse.[158]

We would expect the recipe to claim that Adam Kadmon has come forth again. But the recipe says "old Adam" has come forth, and then

---

[157] *Mysterium Lectures*, p. 257.
[158] *Mysterium Coniunctionis*, par. 611.

it immediately says that "old Adam … Adam Kadmon." Jung suggests that the alchemist must have had a slip of the pen. That slip, however, unconsciously depicts the fact that the redeemed condition is a mixture of both the old and the new. It is not perfection, it is wholeness. Adam Kadmon alone is not an adequate depiction of the end state because it is too perfect. The end state is more realistically a mixture of the new self and the old that brings our humility before us because we are fallible and human like everybody else.

Through crucifixion, the first raw and old Adam is transformed into Adam Kadmon, the embodiment of higher meaning and creative potency. Jung interprets the crucifixion as being splayed on a polarity of four having to do with the four functions of consciousness that see the person's totality. We could also say the cross shows the importance of being suspended between the opposites in the process of rebirth. In any case, the text portrays the transformation from crude to precious, not stated directly, but certainly implied, through the workings of the spirit evoked on the cross of conflict and opposition.

That's Adam. I wanted to give you a taste of the various images the alchemists used and which Jung therefore investigated as the prime symbols for this process of opposition and synthesis in dreams. Throughout the whole of alchemical literature, a broad wealth of metaphors is used to describe an imagined "chemical" process of transformation. The alchemists also saw in a "chemical" process of change a deep spiritual dimension that enriched the depiction of their efforts. Jung studied hundreds of the alchemists' texts—we have just looked at a minuscule sample of them. He then compiled many aspects of the material/spiritual transformation process as those processes are emphasized in the different alchemical texts. Through attentiveness to the alchemists' writings, Jung could gain insight into a wide range of the psychological aspects of the birth of selfhood by interpreting the alchemists' symbolic language of chemical/spiritual change.

In discussing this material, I have been asked, "Where is Eve?" Eve would be the woman's version. The Adam texts are written from a patriarchal perspective, and that's why Eve is not emphasized. We must go to pre-patriarchal sources, for example, for the feminine or female version of psychological processes. (See Appendix Two.) Whether we are discussing male or female psychological growth, the pattern of a raw beginning and a refined end still holds, though the steps and particulars of imagery will vary.

The Three Stages of the Coniunctio

I will summarize the stages, and then we can examine them a bit more closely.

In the final section of *Mysterium,* Jung cites an alchemist named Gerhard Dorn. Dorn was a sixteenth-century alchemist who lived in Basel and Frankfurt, whom Jung held in considerable regard.[159] The passage from Gerhard Dorn that Jung discusses in detail provides us with a very useful point of view:

> "We conclude that meditative philosophy [that's alchemy] consists in the overcoming of the body by mental union (*unio mentalis*). This first union does not as yet make the wise man, but only the mental discipline of wisdom. The second union of the mind with the body shows forth the wise man, hoping for and expecting that blessed third union with the first unity (i.e., the *unus mundus*, the latent unity of the world)."[160]

In Dorn's mind, at the beginning of the alchemists' working with and on some waste or worthless material (the prima materia), there is a spirit inside it. When the alchemist cooks the worthless material, the spirit in it emerges and assumes a separate existence apart from the original material. In the mind of the alchemist, this spirit is sort of floating around inside the vessel that they are cooking, so the result of the cooking produces the original chaos in the worthless material and the spirit that hovers in the vessel as a second presence apart from the first material. In the alchemist's mind, the spirit is a stable,

---

[159] "Gerhard Dorn," Wikipedia, last modified January 22, 2022, https://en.wikipedia.org/wiki/Gerhard_Dorn.
[160] *Mysterium Coniunctionis*, par. 663.

ordering presence.[161] That condition is the *unio mentalis; unio mentalis* means "one mind." A "one mind" is released from the chaos of the worthless material, over and against the chaos of the first material, and brings stability to the conglomeration. Remember, we are working with the understanding of a sixteenth-century mind. This is the first stage. The first stage of union is a separation.

Then, to turn the first material into gold, the spirit has to "come back down again" and join with the first material. This is the second stage. The name of the stage isn't given in the alchemical text we are considering, but the second stage is called the *unio corporalis,* the one body.

In sum: this is Dorn's way of describing the alchemical process. When the spirit separates from the confused mass, that is the *unio mentalis,* the one mind. The alchemists cook the mixture further, and if that is done correctly, the spirit will come back into the confused mass, the *unio corporalis.* When that happens, the mass will turn into gold. All of this takes place in some sort of vessel.

As just mentioned, Jung interprets these alchemical stages metaphorically as depicting what goes on in us during a period and process of psychological transformation. The *unio mentalis* would psychologically equate to our becoming clear about what is going on in our lives and how we feel about that. In the *unio mentalis,* there is objectivity, control, and responsibility—and a little bit of rigidity. Jung interprets the *unio mentalis* as the stage in psychological transformation that is about objectively seeing, having some control over, and taking responsibility for what we do with our emotions. On a psychological level, an example of this distinction would be what I have heard people say who are in AA and are going through the Twelve Steps program. They say that emotions are "just emotions,"

---

[161] Here spirit is used differently than as the force of teleological completion we have been discussing. The spirit here is used closer to the notion of mind, the organizing and clarifying power of conscious understanding. In German, the word *Geist* can mean "spiritual" in the sense of a divine or divine-like presence and potency. It can also mean mental or mind.

and they have to be able to ignore them. This is a critical step in healing from the addiction because the emotions, at this beginning point of recovery, will say things like, "Oh, just have one glass of wine before dinner," or "A quick trip to the massage parlor won't hurt anything." Both moments of enticement lead to relapse. I recall talking with a woman who was in an understandably agitated state after finding out her husband was having an affair. Her therapist told her to go to the lover's house and tell the lover how she felt about the affair. The woman did; she knocked on the door, the lover opened it, the woman told the woman at the door just how she felt about the affair, and then she punched the other woman in the face. Out of that, she lost her job and had to pick up the pieces in an already disheartened state. A *unio mentalis* stage for this woman had not been solidified.

As the *unio mentalis* psychological state is sustained, consciousness can accept experience of the emotions without their being destructive and without having to fastidiously control them—that's the *unio corporalis* stage. In this case, this "spirit" represents the ability of the mind to experience and deal with difficult emotions and *not be controlled by them.*

I imagine that one of the reasons Jung liked Dorn's schema so much is that this second phase is followed by a third phase. The third phase, in the alchemist's mind, is when the *unio corporalis* unites with the world. That union is a mystery. The third stage for Dorn is what Jung would call a synchronicity.

It is not enough to heal personally. We have to take the newly healed condition and put it into the world. Here's the mystery again. We don't just put it into the world; in my experience, *the world also comes to meet us.* This is the third stage, the *unus mundus*, the one world.

This whole schema is a bit of an artificial dissection. Still, we are attempting to conceptualize all the different facets of growth that, in the final analysis, make up transformation at depth. It takes a *response on the part of the world* to give us the right opportunity to place what we have achieved in the world.

The central importance of the third phase, I believe, was what Jung came to at the end of his life.

A great problem is involved with this understanding of psychological transformation in depth. How does the world know to come to us when we are ready? The implication is that there is intelligence in matter itself. There is an intelligence in material events in time and space. Otherwise, how do we explain that at just the right moment, just the right opportunity comes to us from the outer world? Jung and Wolfgang Pauli, the physicist who was part of the discovery of quantum mechanics, had many discussions over just this quandary.[162] Jung recognized that, somehow and at some points, psychological processes are not separate from the outer, material world. It is "as if" the inner psyche draws the world to it. Wolfgang Pauli, who had had considerable Jungian exposure during the course of his life, recognized that the scientific concept of matter is not a holistic one since it has no explanation of how matter can "receive" the activity of inner psychological processes. To deal with this conundrum, many "scientists" call these moments, when inert matter seems to have intelligence, a fantasy or New Age twaddle or flaky spirituality.

These are what Jung calls synchronistic moments. These moments occur, and we say, "How could that have happened?" Just the right relationship opportunity, just the right job opportunity present themselves.

For us to fulfill the meaning that we were put here to fulfill, the world has to be there to fulfill it.

Here is an example. When I was in training, everything went wrong at the beginning. Then, something went right. I was awarded a generous year's fellowship from the Rotary Club in the United States. The deal was that half of the sum would be paid at the beginning of

---

[162] The theme is a running discussion through *Atom and Archetype*.

106

the academic year, and after the appropriate paperwork was submitted halfway through the academic year, at the beginning of the second semester, the second half of the sum would be paid.

I received the first check at the beginning of the fall semester in which I took my series of eight midpoint exams; those exams also started at the beginning of the semester. In those series of eight, I miserably failed my exam on the interpretation of fairy tales with Marie-Louise von Franz. My performance was so bad that she started thumping the table, and at the end of the exam, she told me what I had said was stupid. The worst part was that it *was* stupid.

"That was it," I said to myself as I stomped out of the exam. I was convinced I had made a mistake ever thinking I had what it takes to complete Jungian training. "I quit," I repeated over and over to myself, "this is it; I'm leaving; I'm not meant to be here." As I was fuming and walking with my head down out of the Institute, I passed the little alcove where mail delivered to us by way of the Institute address was placed on a pile. As I walked by that pile of letters, I noticed there was a letter for me *on the top of the pile* of, maybe, forty letters. I grabbed it and started toward the exit. I saw a friend who, of course, had no idea what had just happened. His training, I knew, was going well. He asked me if I wanted to go for a coffee; whereupon, I responded with some heartily nasty words, which I'll spare you.[163] I kept on walking to the street from the Institute and opened the letter. It contained the check for the other half of the fellowship's fund. That check was not supposed to be awarded for another six months and not until a litany of paperwork had been filled out. There it had been in plain sight. I couldn't ignore the message, "Don't give up."

These meaningful moments, these synchronicities, these events where there is convergence between our inner state of mind (in this case) or an inner dream image *and* an event in the outer world, come just when we and the world are in negotiation. That's the third stage of the *coniunctio*. This process opens the door when it is time for our place in the world to be known, received, addressed, and shared.

---

[163] Yes, I later apologized profusely, explaining why I was so upset.

The first stage is developing a strong ego by staying away from the storm of emotions, and the second stage is a strong ego, strong enough to be in touch with the fire of our subjective emotions. There is a going up and then a coming back down. Then a rapport between emotions and thought, feelings and action, can emerge. When the mind comes "back down" again, chaos is moderated. We have less of a tendency to blow up, and we can appropriately express what we are feeling. When emotions and thoughts are working together, *that's when the world brings something to us into which to put the reality of who we are.* That's the third stage of the *unus mundus*, which is often characterized by a "coincidental" event, a synchronicity, which opens doors.

Here's Jung, speaking of synchronistic moments:

> With this conjecture of the *identity of the psychic and the physical* we approach the alchemical view of the *unus mundus* [the one world], the potential world of the first day of creation … .[164]

Jung's idea is that when these synchronicities occur, they are a repetition on a *conscious* level of the early wholeness we are born with and they reappear in time and space through the intervention of matter.

> Microphysics is feeling its way into the unknown side of matter, just as complex psychology [another word for Jungian psychology] is pushing forward into the unknown side of the psyche.[165]

How do these two converge?

> The common background of microphysics and depth psychology is as much physical as psychic and therefore neither, but rather a third thing, a neutral nature which can at most be grasped in hints since in essence it is transcendental. … The transcendental psychophysical background corresponds to a "potential world" in so far as all those conditions which determine the form of empirical phenomena are inherent in it. This

---

[164] *Mysterium Coniunctionis*, par. 766. [emphasis added]
[165] Ibid., par. 768.

obviously holds good as much for physics as for psychology, or, to be more precise, for microphysics as much as for the psychology of consciousness.[166]

Suddenly, we are in very deep water, which challenges our very notion of reality itself.

Jung puts it beautifully:

This much we do know beyond all doubt, that empirical reality has a transcendental background ... .[167]

[166] Ibid., par 768f.
[167] Ibid., par. 768.

AION

The Title *Aion*

Aion is the name of a Mithraic God. Mithraism was a religion that reached its apogee in the Roman Era and was the religion associated with the Roman legions. One of the Gods of Mithraism was called Aion. The Greek word, *aion*, the title Jung chose for his book, is the etymological basis of our word "eon", meaning a long, loosely defined period of time.

Aion was a god of the long duration, often with a common theme or dynamic that defined it. The Greeks had three words for time: *chronos, kairos,* and *aion. Chronos* was the tick-tick-tick of the clock, the space between the ticks, so to speak. *Kairos* was the quality of the moment between the ticks. *Aion* was a long period of time, an epoch. This book is a study of what Jung considers to be the major epochs of Western history, the major eons of Western history, and what that means for us today. Jungian psychology is not just a method of psychotherapy. It is a method of psychotherapy that Jung developed with an eye to what *this historical moment needs*. It is a method coming out of a historic sensitivity. To a large extent, Jung developed his understanding of the process of therapy from history that was based on the unfolding epochs of Western history.

Now we'll examine the book *Aion* passage by passage. I've picked out what I consider the main sentences. If we have an idea of the main points of the book, we will have a first grasp of the overall psychological message of this book.

The Split Christ Image

Several quotes will follow in sequence, then we'll summarize their message.

> There can be no doubt that the original Christian conception of the *imago Dei* [image of God] embodied in Christ meant an all-embracing totality that even includes the animal side of man. Nevertheless the Christ-symbol lacks wholeness in the modern psychological sense, since it does

not include the dark side of things but specifically excludes it in the form of a Luciferian opponent.[168]

The book explores the psychological effect of the Christian understanding of God. It explores the psychological effect on Western history, and thus on us, of the canonical image of Christ. Jung alludes to a split in the Christ image. There is the image of Christ, and there is also the image of the devil. The implication of this for Jung is that the Christian psyche is split if we understand that statement psychologically—split between good and evil.

This theme continues over several paragraphs.

> If we see the traditional figure of Christ as a parallel to the psychic manifestation of the self, then the Antichrist would correspond to the shadow of the self, namely the dark half of the human totality, which ought not to be judged too optimistically. ... In the empirical self, light and shadow form a paradoxical unity. In the Christian concept, on the other hand, the archetype is hopelessly split into two irreconcilable halves, leading ultimately to a metaphysical dualism—the final separation of the kingdom of heaven from the fiery world of the damned.[169]

Jung recognizes that in dreams at depth, the God-images appear as a mixture of opposites contained within a whole—not as two separate polarities, good and evil, as Christendom portrays Christ and Satan. In the standard Christian version, these two are split into two polarities:

> Psychologically the case is clear since the dogmatic figure of Christ is so sublime and spotless that everything else turns dark beside it. It is, in fact, so one-sidedly perfect that it demands a psychic complement to restore the balance.[170]

In Jung's view, this image of God in Christianity, being light in its official theological recognition, sets in motion a counter tendency

---

[168] C.G. Jung, *Aion, The Collected Works of C.G. Jung,* vol. 9ii, par. 74.
[169] Ibid., par. 76.
[170] Ibid., par. 77.

within the Christian society and Christian believer to live out everything that has not been included in the perfect light.

The Historical Split

Soon Jung will take this to history. Human nature is a mixture of opposites, and Christianity only symbolizes the light side of those opposites. Jung wants us to recognize a natural law that there will be an emotional balancing reaction to the light side consisting of a swing to the other, dark side. The Christian image of God introduces an instability into the civilization that worships in the Christian framework.

Why is Jung so concerned about Christianity? He is not indulging in this discussion because Christianity is the "better" religion. It is just that Christianity is the religion that has defined Western civilization. It's not that Judaism is less important or Islam is less important in themselves, but the nature of our Western civilization has been shaped by Christian ideas and images more than by any other religion. Jung is delving into Christianity as a way to understand the Christian civilization and, in turn, how we both make up that civilization and are shaped by it.

Jung puts the point this way:

> The coming of the Antichrist is not just a prophetic prediction—it is an inexorable psychological law ... .[171]

In other words, because Christianity defined God as light, it forced Western civilization into a position of subsequently living out the dark in a period of history.

A main point follows, which is what we've been leading up to.

> A factor that no one has reckoned with, however, is the *fatality inherent in the Christian disposition itself*, which leads inevitably to a reversal of its spirit—not through the obscure workings of chance but in accordance

---

[171] Ibid.

with psychological law. The ideal of spirituality striving for the heights was doomed to clash with the materialistic earth-bound passion to conquer matter and master the world. This change became visible at the time of the "Renaissance." The word means "rebirth," and it referred to the renewal of the antique spirit. We know today that this spirit was chiefly a mask; it was not the spirit of antiquity that was reborn, but the spirit of medieval Christianity that underwent strange pagan transformations, [here are the important words] *exchanging the heavenly goal for an earthly one, and the vertical of the Gothic style for a horizontal perspective (voyages of discovery, exploration of the world and of nature).* The subsequent developments that led to the Enlightenment and the French Revolution have produced a worldwide situation today which can only be called "antichristian" in a sense that confirms the early Christian anticipation of the "end of time."[172]

At the birth of Christianity, Roman antiquity had become so decadent, so self-destructive, in its wanton pursuit of instinctual pleasure (*concupiscentia*) that there had to be a counter-swing away from that depravity in order for civilization to survive. That is what Christianity gave to Western civilization. It provided a spiritual[173] counterpole of control and non-worldly, non-instinctual, non-libidinous, and non-egotistical values. It introduced a value system of light, kindness, grace, and non-worldliness to pull the populace away from the tendency of the Roman Era to destroy itself. That was the valid and healing psychological function of Christianity as far as Jung is concerned. There is a well-founded reason for a God-image, i.e., a Christ-image, that is light and emerged two thousand years ago into our civilization. A pendulum swung from the instinctive brutality of late antiquity to the spiritual grace of Christianity at the birth of Christ. That is represented in the fact that Christ is represented as all spirit, all light, all goodness.

The Christ-image at the birth of Christianity was a necessary shift, in Jung's view. Humanity needed to stabilize, which is why Christianity

---

[172] Ibid., par. 78. [emphasis added]
[173] Spiritual in both senses alluded to in the last chapter. It has to do with the stabilizing impact of certain types of religious experience that uplift— and the understanding of that uplifting as orienting to higher, and non-bodily, values.

commanded so much power. A spiritual first eon, was introduced into Western history, a spiritual first *aion,* to use the title of the book we are considering. Jung looks at the two poles of the God-image and the two understandings of human nature that run alongside it. He then applies the polarity recognition to the sweep of Western history. The first eon of Western history, which lasted about a thousand years, was a spiritual eon. The establishment of monasteries, the propagation of Christendom, and the non-worldly character of the Middle Ages held sway for about a thousand years.

The spiritual movement is one pole of a pendulum swing. Since it embodied only one-half of human nature, the pendulum swing had to reverse in the other direction to balance out the one-sided characteristics of the first swing to the spirit. The balancing movement of the pendulum was toward a materialistic, worldly, power-oriented, and secular set of values and lifestyles. That is what we see in the Renaissance, where the spirituality of the Middle Ages became the worldliness of Medici Florence. The scientific revolution is part of this swing that put matter at the focus of our interests. The Age of Exploration and its subsequent imperialism is also relevant here. The pendulum swing moved away from a heavenly spirit and toward a worldly order of matter.

For Jung, those two poles of a pendulum swing have made up Western history from the time of Christ until now.[174] The two poles consist of a spiritual phase and a material phase; a non-worldly phase and a worldly phase; a religious phase and a secular phase; a phase of grace and a phase of conquering; a phase of prayer and a phase of exploration—a spiritual phase of the first thousand years and a material phase of the next thousand years. Jung sees contradictory tendencies as inherent, not only in our Western Christian-stamped

[174] Although Jung was intensely interested in Asia's religious and cultural contributions to Western life, with respect to the events of history and with respect to his historical period, his primary concern was European history and that of the Western hemisphere. In this third millennium, world history can no longer be broken down into West and East. Understanding historical events from this wider perspective remains uncharted territory in Jungian inquiry—and stands as one of its most pressing challenges.

civilization but also in the typical Christian personality that is characterized by the same split—represented by the light Christ and the devil.

Aion is about the two major eons of Western civilization characterized by the pendulum swing toward opposites that have made up our history so far. This historical split is why Jung titled his book *Aion*.

Synthesis

Why should we care? Because we are living in the time of another pendulum swing. The first thousand years were a spiritual phase; the second thousand years were a material phase. We are now beginning another thousand-year period, which Jung understands as bringing the need to synthesize the two extremes. It is the task of our time to mitigate the pendulum swings. This is what Jung focuses on for the remainder of his book *Aion*.

I understand that Jungian psychology is based on a methodology that tries to pay attention to this synthesis, this unity between, or unification of, spirit and matter. The Jungian approach seeks to unify the psychological impact of the spiritual emphasis of the first eon of our history and the psychological impact of the material emphasis of the second eon of our history. We work hard not to single out the spirit. We don't single out the material world. Religious counseling would single out the spirit as primary. Psychoanalytic, secular psychology would single out the material, the instincts, and the here-and-now as the primary focus. Jung responds to this by observing that either of those, by itself, is simply propagating the old split. He thus tried to find a way to stop the pendulum swing on an individual basis. If these efforts can occur on an individual basis, this will be a first step in stopping the massive swings on a societal scale.

Two Fish

Jung examines the way this split and synthesis has been symbolized in Western culture—we are again touching on our old friend's alchemy. He investigates how we are likely to see these dynamics in an individual's dreams. And when we see the dynamics symbolized in our dreams, what are we to do about it?

He next observes how closely linked fish symbolism is connected to the figure of Christ. He then examines an aspect of astrological symbolism in this Christian context.

> In view of this wide distribution of the fish symbol its appearance at a particular place or at a particular moment in the history of the world is no cause for wonder. But the sudden activation of the symbol, and its identification with Christ even in the early days of the Church, lead one to conjecture a second source. This source is astrology … .[175]

In order to digest Jung's reference to this second source, we need to understand what astronomers and astrologers mean by the *spring point*.

When the sun rises on the first day of spring, the astronomical and astrological constellation that can be seen in the background of the sun at the very moment of its rising is called the spring point. The background constellation changes very slowly over time. It takes a bit more than two thousand years for the constellation in back of the rising sun on the first day of spring to change from one constellation to the next. Today, at the beginning of the twenty-first century, the sun is seen to rise just at the end edge of the constellation Pisces and just at the beginning edge of the constellation Aquarius. For the last 2000 years, the sun was seen against the backdrop of the constellation Pisces when it rose on the first day of spring. Now it is beginning to be seen against the backdrop of the constellation of Aquarius. The astronomy which explains this fact need not occupy us; it has to do

---

[175] *Aion*, par. 128.

with a peculiarity in the motion of the earth.[176] The important point is the shift of the spring point through the constellations of the heavens with each shift taking roughly 2000 years from constellation to constellation. (See figure 8.)

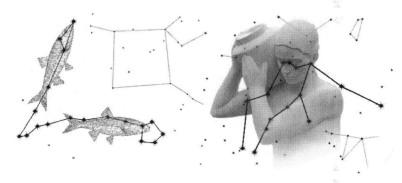

Figure 8

Jung's discussion pays particular attention to the fact that over the last 2000 years, the spring point has moved through the constellation of Pisces. In other words, over the last 2000 years, the sun was seen, at sunrise, with the constellation Pisces in its background. At the time of the birth of Christ, the background of the rising sun was at the beginning of the constellation Pisces. At the end of the twentieth century, it was seen at the end of the constellation Pisces. Today the background is the beginning of the constellation Aquarius.[177]

The constellation of Pisces is represented by two fish. This fact occupied Jung's attention. He was especially interested that the first fish of Pisces is represented in a vertical orientation, and the second fish of Pisces is represented in a horizontal orientation.

Jung notes the coincidence that fish symbolism plays such a big role in Christianity and that Christianity, astrologically speaking, was born just at the beginning of the constellation of Pisces when the

---

[176] In astronomical terms, the *precession* (very, very, very slow wobble) of the axis of the earth.

[177] Sung out proudly in "Aquarius" from the musical *Hair*.

spring point was just at the beginning of the constellation Pisces. The presence of fish symbolism in Christianity that coincides with the presence of fish symbolism in the Age of Pisces struck Jung as intensely meaningful.

Compare the discussion concerning the two periods of Western history with the fish symbolism of the constellation of Pisces. Jung contends there has been a spiritual (vertical) phase of history and a material (horizontal) period of history. Jung observes a coincidence in the symbolism between the first (spiritual) thousand years of history as being simultaneous with the vertical fish and the second (material) thousand years of history as being simultaneous with the horizontal fish. Jung senses an influence of Christian symbolism on history—or at least a parallel between Christian symbolism and history.

This is such a different way of understanding that it will take a minute to repeat and digest. The first thousand-year period of Western civilization was a spiritual one—characterized by the growth of monasteries and the flowering of religious cults. The second thousand-year period of Western civilization is a material one—characterized by the Age of Exploration, the Renaissance, the Reformation, the Enlightenment, the birth of science, and all the revolutions establishing a secular government up until today. We are living at the end of that second period of history where the swing from vertical to horizontal has taken place and has been lived out. *Now our task is, I emphasize, to unite the two swings, emblemized by those two fish in astrological imagery, in a single attitude.*

This synthesis is the problem and challenge of our time:

If, as seems probable, the aeon of the fishes [that's why we examined the themes of the two eons] is ruled by the archetypal motif of the hostile brothers [meaning the two fish moving in different directions in their astrological portrayal], then the approach of the next Platonic month,[178]

---

[178] The period of time marked out by each astrological sign, about two thousand years.

namely Aquarius, *will constellate the problem of the union of opposites*.[179]

The psychological task of our time is to begin to unite these two opposites of spirit and matter that have been lived out sequentially. Now they are to be lived out as a challenge to synthesis.

> It will then no longer be possible to write off evil as the mere privation of good; its real existence will have to be recognized. This problem can be solved neither by philosophy, nor by economics, nor by politics, but only by the individual human being, via his experience of the living spirit.[180]

The psychological task is now to unite spirit (the vertical) and matter (the horizontal), while up to now, the two poles have been lived out first as spirit and then as matter. It is all pertinent to the way we do Jungian therapy. Jung's approach in the consulting room is based on a carefully articulated historical understanding.

He sums up what he is saying:

> Although no connection of any kind can be proved between the figure of Christ and the inception of the astrological age of the fishes, the simultaneity [that's the big word] of the fish symbolism of the Redeemer with the astrological symbol of the new aeon seems to me important enough to warrant the emphasis we place upon it. If we try to follow up the complicated mythological ramifications of this parallel, we do so with intent to throw light on the multifarious aspects of an archetype that manifests itself on the one hand in a personality, and on the other hand synchronistically, [that is] in a moment of time determined in advance, before Christ's birth.[181]

This theme of uniting the opposites, and indeed fish symbols representing the unity of opposites, is occurring in the individual in the same way it occurs thematically in the astrological conception of things. Again, in the same way, the theme of opposites and their

---

[179] *Aion*, par. 142. [emphasis added]
[180] Ibid.
[181] Ibid., par. 148.

unification is being played out in historical patterns, according to Jung's view. This, of course, takes place in people without knowledge of Jungian psychology. It's just a coincidence Jung noticed and then proceeded to take it seriously. We see these parallel themes in individuals, in astrology, in the Christ image, and within history.

> It becomes a matter for astonishment only when, through the precession of the equinoxes, the spring-point moves into this sign [Pisces] and thus inaugurates an age in which the "fish" was used as a name for the God who became a man, who was born as a fish and was sacrificed as a ram, who had fishermen for disciples and wanted to make them fishers of men, who fed the multitude with miraculously multiplying fishes, who was himself eaten as a fish, the "holier food," and whose followers are little fishes, the "pisciculi."[182]

> The northerly, or easterly, fish [that's the vertical fish], which the spring-point entered at about the beginning of our era, is joined to the southerly, or westerly, fish [the horizontal fish] by the so-called commissure. This consists of a band of faint stars forming the middle sector of the constellation, and the spring-point gradually moved along its southern edge. The point where the ecliptic intersects with the meridian at the tail of the second fish coincides roughly with the sixteenth century, the time of the Reformation, which as we know is so extraordinarily important for the history of Western symbols. Since then the spring-point has moved along the southern edge of the second fish, and will enter Aquarius in the course of the third millennium [which is us, now]. Astrologically interpreted, the designation of Christ as one of the fishes identifies him with the first fish, the vertical one. Christ is followed by the Antichrist, at the end of time. The beginning of the enantiodromia [swinging into its opposite] would fall, logically, midway between the two fishes. We have seen that this is so. The time of the Renaissance begins in the immediate vicinity of the second fish, and with it comes that spirit which culminates in the modern age.[183]

So how do we unite spirit and matter?

---

[182] Ibid.
[183] Ibid., par. 149.

The Second Fish

To that end, Jung next psychologically analyzes on a personal level what he has just discussed from a historical perspective: the nature of the second fish for an individual's inner journey. *He finds the way we unite spirit and matter* is to start with the meaning of the second fish in our lives because the second fish defines our time. *The psychological task of our time is to extract/pluck the spirit out of the second fish, so to speak.* Where religion starts with the spirit, Jung starts with matter. The second fish is our starting point. How do we get spirit out of the second fish as matter? What does that mean for therapy? The discussion becomes practical in its application to the inner journey in analysis. Jung's focus has evolved from the implied duality of Christ (Christ and Satan) to the two periods of history to the duality of fish symbolism, to the synthesis of that duality, and finally, to what this all means for the practice of analysis.[184]

Jung methodically looks at the way fish has been described in tradition. Certainly, at the time of Christ, this is relevant.

> *Concupiscentia* is attributed to fishes, which are said to be "ambitious, libidinous, voracious, avaricious, lascivious"—in short, an emblem of the vanity of the world and of earthly pleasures … .[185]

---

[184] Jung has shifted from a historical to a personal perspective here. It's in the individual that he feels, at least for the present, that the unification can occur. Earlier, we saw: "That the consciousness of … individuality should coincide exactly with the reactivation of an archaic god-image is … a very frequent occurrence which, in my view, corresponds to an unconscious law." [C.G. Jung, "The Relations between the Ego and the Unconscious," *Two Essays on Analytical Psychology, The Collected Works of C.G. Jung*, vol. 7, par. 248.] As the Self is not infrequently symbolized by images of God, Jung at times uses the term God-image to refer to the Self. Why this link between the Self and the God-image? For Jung, this is just the way we are made. So individual work on the split in our own internal Self, in our inner God-image, is at the same time a step in the direction of healing the general religious split in history's previous dangerously simplistic (mis)understanding of God.

[185] *Aion*, par. 174.

On the one hand, the fish is an image of greed and lust. As Jung says of the fish:

They owe these bad qualities most of all to their relationship with the mother- and love-goddess Ishtar, Astarte, Atargatis, or Aphrodite.[186]

That is the way the mother goddess was interpreted in a patriarchal framework.

On the other hand, Jung observes:

Christ is not only a fisher but the fish that is "eucharistically" eaten. Augustine says in his *Confessions*: "But [the earth] eats the fish that was drawn from the deep, at the table which you have prepared for them that believe; for the fish was drawn from the deep in order to nourish the needy ones of the earth."[187]

Two senses of the fish show up in its mythological precedent and reflect the discussion of the vertical and horizontal fish. One sense is that it represents greed; the other is that it indicates spirit.

We have concluded that the implied duality of the Christ image, the two meanings of the fish, is to be synthesized in our time. Then if one side is recognized as greed and the other side is to be taken as the guiding spirit, the synthesis of the two will be *to find the guiding spirit embedded within the wildness of greed.* From this, Jung examines how we can find the spirit within what has traditionally been called *concupiscentia.* Uniting the opposites in this sense is, in other words, finding the spiritual fish within the material fish. Put differently, we turn to the greed aspect of life and find in it the spirit aspect of life, the inner guidance, the spirit, which has been the leitmotif of Jung's psychology since 1912. When I say the greed aspect of life, I mean desire, ambition, libidinous states of mind, voraciousness, avarice, lasciviousness—the whole physiological, desirous side of life, including the workings of our body. When I say spirit, I mean, and it's worth repeating:

---

[186] Ibid.
[187] Ibid.

That factor that creates images in the inner field of vision [in other words, creates dreams and fantasies] and organizes [that's the key word here] them into a meaningful order.[188]

So, when we endure the ordeal of cooking in our passions, the second fish, then we can watch how when we have understood one dream, the next dream is a step ahead of the previous dream. We are thereby guided—the guidance the first fish represents. This guidance in us, Jung calls "spirit." That spirit is embedded in us just as much as our passions are—something moralists are incapable of understanding.[189] The way we can be guided by it is to maintain the awareness of our instincts, the second fish, and their proclivity to evolve.

True to his method, Jung looks to other traditions where a redeemer is transformed from a low state. He looks at the symbolism of the fish—on the one hand being *concupiscentia* and on the other hand as containing the possibility of the purity of Christ or the Messiah.

> According to the Syrian Apocalypse of Baruch, Leviathan shall rise from the sea with the advent of the Messiah.[190]

---

[188] As Marie-Louise von Franz's words have beautifully contributed to our discussion, from *Number and Time*, p. 214.

[189] I'll always remember Dr. Conrad Bonifazi, my theology professor in divinity school, saying, "Moralists have the dirtiest minds, they see filth everywhere."

[190] *Aion*, par. 178.

Here is a picture of Leviathan by William Blake. (See figure 9.) Leviathan occurs in several places in the Bible. One place the monster appears is in the Book of Job. Leviathan is a sea monster fish, and Behemoth is a land monster. So, Leviathan, as the fish in a negative version, is going to come up out of the water at the advent of the Messiah and become the foundation of the Eucharist. Hence Jung:

> According to the Apocalypse of Baruch, Behemoth as well as Leviathan is a Eucharistic food.[191]

Figure 9

The Apocalypse of Baruch is Jewish apocalyptic and apocryphal literature. In that account, the fish that returns is a negative fish. It's the fish that represents everything we are not supposed to be. That negative fish becomes the Host. Psychologically understood, this is another representation of the extraction of an end state from an unsavory, even heinous, beginning.

The healing event, the synthesis, is when that negative fish, the fish as *concupiscentia*, becomes a sacred meal. Or in psychological language, the healing event, the synthesis, is when the second fish becomes the vehicle for ascertaining the spirit. *That, in a nutshell, is the point of* Aion.

The problem the current Christian eon has given us is confronting the material excess from the last thousand years and finding the spirit embedded in it. The dangers are that the dark side is simply

---

[191] Ibid., par. 181.

disregarded as dark, and the spirit is approached separately from matter. When I say matter, I refer to the sense of greed already noted, the crude sulphur—to use a term discussed previously—onslaught on our lives from the material sphere. That spirit as guidance is in the background of everything we've entertained in our attentiveness to Jung's major works: Where is our inner guidance? How do we find it? That is another way of asking: Where is our spirit? What is our spirit doing? How can I create my genuine future? And how can I bring my instincts along with it?

Jung has presented us with such a new and novel viewpoint that a quick recap is in order. The basic idea has been the split in the God-image has shaped our civilization. A telling detail here is the coincidence of astrological symbolism paralleling our understanding of the psychological influence of Christianity, which introduced the image of the two fish into the discussion—the vertical fish and the horizontal fish. The image of fish or fishes is one of the ways this theme shows up in dreams. We'll now look at the nature of the second fish and talk about the horizontal fish (materiality) as the way to synthesis.

The Fish in Alchemy

Jung considers the role of the fish image in alchemy with considerable care. He begins this way:

> The text containing the earliest reference to the fish [in alchemy] runs: "There is in the sea a round fish, lacking bones and cortex, and having in itself a fatness, a wondrous virtue, which, if it is cooked on a slow fire until its fatness and moisture entirely disappear ... is saturated with sea-water until it begins to shine.[192]

Then he explicates:

> This round fish is certainly not a fish in the modern sense, but an invertebrate [no skeletal structure]. This is borne out by the absence of bones and "cortex," which in medieval Latin simply means a

---

[192] Ibid., par. 195.

musselshell or mollusc. At all events, it is some kind of round organism that lives in the sea, presumably a scyphomedusa or jellyfish ... .[193]

The first reference to a fish in alchemy is to a jellyfish. Recall alchemical texts are alchemical recipes. The alchemist either "sees" a jellyfish in his alchemical cooking vessel, or he may literally fetch a jellyfish from the ocean and start his alchemical work on that actual organism. In any case, that imagined or real fish would be cooked; it absorbs water and begins to glow in the alchemist's mind. What interests Jung is the reference to glowing.

He continues:

> Our text remarks that when the "round fish" is warmed or cooked on a slow fire it "begins to shine." In other words, the heat already present in it becomes visible as light. ... This fish was said to be hot and burning, and to consume as with fire everything it touched in the sea.[194]

Jung cites another author writing about a different fish. As we have seen, he follows this method since there is a thematic parallel between the two alchemists' writings. He is thinking thematically, not linearly.

> This fish, says our author inconsequently, burns but gives no light.[195]

It's from recipes like this that Jung found confirmation of his recognition of the second fish as the portal to the spirit. In these alchemical descriptions of the fish, heat is seen within the fish that, if properly treated by just the right alchemical procedure, turns into light. Light, psychologically speaking, would be the understanding that we talked about—the guidance we are trying to get out of a difficult psychological or physiological point of suffering.

The burning but giving no light would equate to the fact that these emotional desires and experiences are hot and passionate, but they

---

[193] Ibid., par 196.
[194] Ibid., par. 197.
[195] Ibid., par. 199.

don't communicate their understanding until we know how to work on them.

This jellyfish image was significant to Jung. As he cites this dream, he does not provide the information that it is his own dream, although he does state this in *Memories, Dreams, Reflections*.[196] Jung had the dream when he was 18 or 19 years old when he was trying to decide what to do with his life. He drew one conclusion for us in this telling. He likely drew an additional conclusion for himself.

> "He dreamt [he really means 'I dreamt'] that he was walking in a wood. Gradually this grew more and more lonely and wild, and finally he realized that he was in a primeval forest. The trees were so high and the foliage so thick that it was almost dark on the ground. All trace of a path had long since disappeared, but, driven on by a vague sense of expectation and curiosity, he pressed forward and soon came to a circular pool, measuring ten to twelve feet across. It was a spring, and the crystal-clear water looked almost black in the dark shadows of the trees. In the middle of the pool there floated a pearly organism, about eighteen inches in diameter, that emitted a faint light. It was a jelly-fish."[197]

Jung says in *Aion* and in *Memories, Dreams, Reflections*, that because the image was in and of nature, the dream led him to feel that his calling was to study science. In both texts, he observes that his dream led him to study science. That is a valid statement, of course,[198] but there is probably a lot more to say. The atmosphere of the dream is dark; note that he's left any path. The mythology of the jellyfish just noted is that it burns but gives no light. That also tells us, I'd suggest, that Jung would have to go through a lot of burning to be able to create Jungian psychology. So, yes, the nature reference would have to do with his deciding to study nature, insofar as medicine examines the natural life of the body. But it also shows that the light he would produce, the illumination Jungian psychology has provided us, and the insights that Jung provided into our person and our time came to Jung through the emotional fire of passionate burning. That is often the way genuine creativity works. It is

---

[196] C. G. Jung, *Memories, Dreams, Reflections*, p. 85.
[197] *Aion*, par. 208.
[198] Ibid., *Memories, Dreams, Reflections*, p. 85.

preceded by a rough road of desire until we feel we can't take it any longer. Finally, if the person's maturity is up to the ordeal, this leads to understanding and creation.

One of my favorite quotes from an alchemical writer is as follows:

"Hell is a system of upper powers reflected in the lower ... ."[199]

"Hell" here would refer to suffering, misery on Earth, frustration, unfulfilled hopes, desires, complicated situations, love triangles, bankruptcies, car accidents. Think about how bad physical life on Earth can get. That's hell.

"System of upper powers" refers to the spirit. In other words, it refers to the future plan of our life, the knowledge to get our development to where we need to go, and the guiding function to direct us on how to complete our lives.

The issues that we are suffering through contain the kernel of our future development. The hell we are going through, in a symbolic way, contains a message concerning how our lives can develop now and into the future. Life's difficulties, if we know how to receive them and understand their message, can communicate how our lives can most meaningfully develop. The difficulties are containers for the spirit knowledge.

The other implication of the quote is in the word "system." In Jung's view, this spirit that we have talked about, the knowledge that has the capacity to create the future, speaks from the inborn knowledge of who we are in a complete sense. The system of our identity is given to us piece by piece. We get it piece by piece, but the whole, which we get in small doses, does exist as a whole, somehow beyond time and space. The pattern of who we are exists prior to us; it's there when we are born. It's as if to get itself known, the pattern trickles down to earth and, at times, makes the most awful messes. In unraveling these messes, we find out who we are.

---

[199] *Aion*, par. 209.

The quote embodies the fact, which is abundantly clear to me, that there is a purpose to our life. Each word in the quote is very carefully chosen to express how purpose works. Events are often purposed in the way the quote describes.

Magnetism

Jung broadens the discussion:

> In a treatise of the seventeenth century, by an anonymous French author, our strange hybrid, the "round fish," finally becomes a verifiable vertebrate known to zoology: *Echeneis remora*, the common remora or sucking-fish. It belongs to the mackerel family, and is distinguished by a large, flat, oval-shaped sucker on the top of the head in place of the dorsal fin. By means of this it attaches itself either to a larger fish or to a ship's bottom and in this wise is transported about the world.[200]

The text says of the fish:

> "This little fish is extremely small, alone, and unique in its shape, but the sea is great and vast, and hence it is impossible for those to catch it who do not know in what part of the world it dwells. ... The little fish called Remora ... is able to hold back the proud vessels of the great Ocean sea (that is the spirit of the world). Those who are not sons of the art are altogether ignorant and know not those precious treasures which are concealed by nature in the precious and heavenly Aqua Vitae of our sea. ... I instruct you concerning the magnet of the wise [he is introducing a new term into the discussion], which has the power of attracting the little fish called Echeneis or Remora from out [of] the centre and depth of the sea. If it is caught in accordance with nature ... ."[201]

The main point here is a bit involved. The idea implied in the fish sucking on the boats and slowing them down is that the fish exerts a kind of magnetic field on the ship. Remember, this is in the medieval mind. To catch that fish, another magnetic field capable of counteracting the disturbing magnetic field of the fish on ships is

---

[200] Ibid., par 217.
[201] Ibid., par 218.

necessary. That is what the comment in the text, "accordance with nature," refers to. Another magnetism catches the "magnetic" fish. This other magnetism catching the Remora fish according to nature implies a magnetism is needed to catch the magnetism of the fish that slows down ships. In jumbled statements like this, we always have to recall that we are dealing with medieval thinking, and we have to sort out medieval thinking in a way we can make sense of.

That "capturing" magnet is a way of understanding and requires an explanation.

Remember that we experience what the (second) fish symbolizes as being an instinct or strong desire or passionately chaotic state of mind—or as being caught up in some (usually) messy situation that we got into with the "help" of some instinct or desire or state of mind. That "fish energy" in the unconscious has power to exert control over us and drag us down as a magnet pulls on a piece of iron. Jung interprets this by analogy. He seizes on the image of a magnetic fish as an allegory of what goes on in the psyche during a particular phase of a psychological process. When the alchemists, in their allegorical mind, say that these fish slow ships down, Jung, in his allegorical mind, understands that statement to represent the fact that problematic unconscious content can interfere with the way we live our lives. Then, the alchemist says, to counteract the magnetic force between the fish and the ship, another magnetic force has to be applied. That applied magnetic and countering force, which the alchemists called a "magnet of wisdom," is necessary to capture the Echeneis Remora fish. In the alchemist's mind, wisdom is analogous to a magnet; it has attracting power. Now, transfer these analogies to psychology. There is a magnetic aspect to the complexes that disturb us. The complex slows us down by grabbing onto us. A "magnet of wisdom" is necessary for us to begin to have an effect on breaking the "magnetic" hold of a complex over our life. That "magnet of wisdom," Jung suggests, is a particular way of understanding, and that way of understanding is symbolic. It's like there is a "symbolic receptor" in a complex that needs a symbolic way of understanding on the part of consciousness to have an effect on the complex and to begin to neutralize its often pernicious hold on the way we think, feel, and live. We have to find the metaphor within the complex itself and bring the correct metaphoric understanding to our attempts to harness the complex under the control of consciousness. Put differently, something about the unconscious complexes works symbolically, and our mind must approach it with a symbolic capacity of understanding that resonates with the "something-about-the-unconscious complex" that works symbolically. We have to be able to work symbolically to give the symbolic nature of the complex the adequate framework for being understood in our consciousness. The complex speaks in symbols, and we must be intimate with symbolism to understand it. The complex has its own means of expression, and we have to grasp its unique way of understanding to receive that understanding. It's as if our mind has to be able to pull the understanding of the unconscious into consciousness as a magnet pulls in iron particles.

There is more on the magnetic field and the Echeneis:

> We shall now turn to the problem raised by the anonymous French author of the "Instructio de arbore solari," the problem of how the fish is caught. The Echeneis exercises an attraction on ships that could best be compared with the influence of a magnet on iron. [As we have seen.] The attraction, so the historical tradition says, emanates from the fish and brings the vessel, whether powered by sail or oarsmen, to a standstill. I mention this seemingly unimportant feature because, as we shall see, in the alchemical view the attraction no longer proceeds from the fish but from a magnet which man possesses and which exerts the attraction that was once the mysterious property of the fish.[202]

As noted, we must have the magnet to counteract the fish's magnet. That's what symbolic understanding does.

> It is therefore a remarkable innovation when the alchemists set out to manipulate an instrument that would exert the same powers as the Echeneis, but on the Echeneis itself. This reversal of direction is important for the psychology of alchemy because it offers a parallel to the adept's claim to be able to produce the *filius macrocosmi* [the son of the macrocosm, that would be the goal of the work], the equivalent of

---

[202] Ibid., par. 239.

Christ—*Deo concedente* [God willing]—through his art. In this way the artifex or his instrument comes to replace the Echeneis and everything it stood for as the arcane [obscure, initial] substance. He has, so to speak, inveigled the secret out of the fish and seeks to draw the arcane substance to the surface in order to prepare from it the *filius philosophorum*, the *lapis* [the son of the philosophers, the valuable stone, other words for the goal of the work].[203]

Jung emphasizes why he feels a familiarity with symbolism is so important. The contents of the unconscious operate symbolically, so we have to understand symbolism to capture the meaning of what is occurring in our depths. Our grasp of symbolic language neutralizes the power of the unconscious and its affinity to symbolism with that same symbolism. At its most practical, the issue is that we need familiarity with the mythological background of the dream image in order to relate to the dream image.

The magnet of the wise, as a way of understanding, is teachable:

> The "magnet of the wise" which is to draw the wonder-working fish to the surface can, our text says, be *taught*. The content of this secret teaching is the real arcanum [secret] of alchemy.[204]

Jung's discussion now proceeds from the symbolism of the magnet to the symbolism of water. In this, he is again following the medieval mind of the alchemists who held there is a connection between the magnet and wisdom that can be taught. Its effects can bring the "wonderful" fish to the surface (the fish as raw material transformed into a healing elixir by their efforts in the laboratory). For Jung, this power of the magnet/wisdom has to do with the power of symbolic understanding. The alchemists, as well, held there is also a meaningful link between *water* and symbolic understanding. For them, water, in this context, is the water doctrine of the Church. This is not as far-fetched as it sounds because Origen, a Church Father of the third century, said the same thing.[205] The water of ecclesiastical truth, the alchemists would acknowledge from Origen, washes the

---

[203] Ibid.
[204] Ibid., par. 240.
[205] Edward Edinger, *The Aion Lectures*, p. 123.

132

believer in the truths that the Church holds sacred. The alchemists simply extend that to mean the "doctrine" of alchemical imagery and reflection, depicting and explaining transformation with a power analogous to the water of doctrine of the Church, possess truths that the alchemists need to complete their alchemical opus on base material.[206] As with the magnet, for Jung the water of doctrine in alchemy has to do with the effectiveness of symbolic understanding. Symbolic truth, magnetism, and water—as confusing as this is to the modern, linear mind—all refer to the selfsame experience of symbolic imagery's potency to convey truths about life that are beyond the capacity of "normal" rational thinking to approach.

Swimming

Pisces is the *aion* of the two fish, as we've seen. Fish swim in water. Fish are contained in water. The symbolic representation of the last eon is fish contained in water. This representation equates to the believer getting in touch with the symbolic life through the Church. It is a not-infrequent dream theme today that containers of water are breaking. Or even more vividly, there are dreams of a container of water that holds fish, an aquarium for example, and that container has broken. The fish that were once held in it are gasping for air on the floor. This corresponds to the uncomfortable fact that for more and more people, their religious container is collapsing. The ability of the soul to be contained in the water of believing through the Church has become painfully elusive. Increasing numbers of persons are *not* contained in the Church. The world is full of souls that are at loose ends, lost in a wilderness of meaningless events, unable to feel their core supported and nourished by meaningful images, believable truths, and significant experience.

The fish no longer contained in water, so to speak, comes at the end of the Age of Pisces, the end of the eon of containment. The water of containment is gone. It is no wonder that if we take the imagery of Pisces as a metaphor for our time, as the last eon ends, more people are lost.

---

[206] *Aion*, pars. 243f., *Mysterium Coniunctionis*, par. 372.

The imagery of the next eon, the Age of Aquarius, Jung understands as a healing image for the confusion at the end of Pisces.

The task of the next eon, the Aquarian age, depicted as the water carrier, is not only that we extract spirit from the second fish but that *we carry the water that contains the fish*. Where previously, the fish were contained in water, the psychological task visiting us now in the transition of eons is to hold the water that contains the fish. Practically that means that we find the mythological or religious images and powers within ourselves. We turn to the reality of the symbolic world and relate to it within ourselves. We do not look outside us for the authoritative voices that guide us. We hear those voices, submit to their messages, and let them be our guide. We are dealing with a fundamental shift in consciousness. This is the inner guidance, the true living spirit, as Jung repeatedly points out while elucidating the processes of transformation at depth.

The water that once contained us has to become our possession. The fish swam in the water in Pisces. Aquarius, identified as the water carrier, carries that water. We are now responsible for the symbolic world that previous generations lived through participation in the Church. We have to withdraw the projections previous generations put on religious iconography and find an individual relationship internally to what we once found only on the outside.

Gnostic Model of the Self

In the last part of *Aion*,[207] Jung begins discussing a model for the Self drawn from Gnostic imagery. I'm going to explain this part of the book in brief. Jung's descriptions become highly intricate. He dives into fine points of symbolism that can be overwhelming. It will be sufficient to grasp Jung's main intent and not become sidetracked by the various detailed aspects of his overall observations in this section. At first reading, the following paragraph will seem senseless, but with unpacking, it will make sense. (See figure 10.)[208]

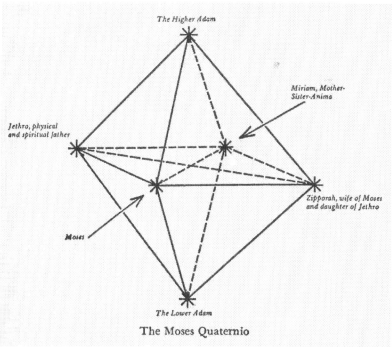

The Moses Quaternio

Figure 10

"The Naassenes [a Gnostic sect], as Hippolytus [a Christian writer who described the theology of the Gnostics, as he sought to discredit them] says, derived all things from a triad, which consists firstly of the 'blessed

---

[207] *Aion*, chapter XIV.
[208] Ibid., p. 227.

135

nature of the blessed Man on high, Adamas,' secondly of the mortal nature of the lower man, and thirdly of the 'kingless race begotten from above,' to which belong 'Mariam the sought-for one, and Jothor the great wise one, and Sephora the seer, and Moses whose generation was not in Egypt.'"[209]

In the last part of *Aion,* Jung shows how the Self evolves over time. He begins with the statement from Gnosticism that holds there is a development between a lower man and a higher man by way of four points which are represented by the four characters mentioned in the writings of Hippolytus.[210] The names of those four characters in the diagram are not important for understanding Jung's discussion. Important for us is that Jung recognizes that we start with the second fish. In the current passage, the lower man is tantamount to the second fish in our previous discussion—the problematic fish in its first chaotic appearance. We work on it. We end up with an insight and a sense of our life that is "higher" and more stable or more consistent, more encompassing—the state that evolves from our psychological efforts.

What we have not talked about until now is the "in-between," between the initial chaos and the resolution in terms of the healed condition in touch with greater inner wisdom. Often the initial state will break up into a quaternity of conflicting elements, which in time resolve into a complete image.

---

[209] Ibid., par. 328.

[210] It's a detail, but one worth noting. The original texts of the Gnostics were unknown to us until 1945 when a whole cache of original Gnostic texts that had been buried for millennia were discovered in Egypt near the town of Nag Hammadi. The original texts were, thus, not available to Jung. A third-century Church Father, Hippolytus, wrote an extensive polemic against the Gnostics in which he copiously quoted their texts, in order to critique them. These were the texts available to Jung. After the discovery of the Nag Hammadi manuscripts, it could be confirmed that Hippolytus' quoting of the texts he was protesting against was quite accurate. So the sources that Jung cites from Hippolytus are accurate to the originals.

Jung is adding complexity to our original discussion. Until now, we have just observed, "We go from a second fish to a higher understanding of ourselves as we extract the spirit, the first fish, from the second fish." Or we face the duality of our conflict in the chaos assaulting us until a synthesis emerges.[211] Now Jung is showing how what we find in the second fish as we seek to recognize the spirit / first fish within it can be made up of several components.

Why Adam? Adam surprisingly shows up in dreams because, I suppose, in our tradition, Adam is the first person. So, Adam stands for an initial condition of raw nature, raw desire, and raw emotions. In other words, the shift from the second fish to the redeemed condition often goes through a period of conflict in which the initial chaotic beginning can also be symbolized as an Adam figure. The initial state of the second fish is Adam. Then development proceeds by way of a conflict.

Why is that important? Because sometimes we don't get an image of that second fish. We get an image of four things in conflict that are contained in the second fish or in an Adam figure.

In the rest of the book, Jung says that this development from an initial state to a completed state can occur at many different points in life. Sometimes the beginning is depicted in fish imagery; sometimes the beginning is depicted as a human being, sometimes as a rock, sometimes as an animal, and sometimes as a vegetable.

Jung then examines four different symbol systems that this process of transformation can be expressed in. Don't be concerned about all of the varieties of symbols at the moment. Just be aware that Jung is showing this shift from beginning to end through one–four–one symbolism. This shift can have a little more complicated presentation than what he has been presenting up to this point in *Aion*. The point is to realize that the one–four–one can occur in a whole range of images: fish, vegetables, stones, people … whatever. The details of

---

[211] As was discussed in the chapters on *Mysterium Coniunctionis*.

137

the transformation are a little bit different in each case, but for our intermediate purposes, all we need to remember is one–four–one.

The Cycle

The other point Jung makes at the end of the book is that this one–four–one process is a cycle. We generally begin with a "low" image of the starting condition, say a rock or a fish. The next cycle may have a "higher" image on the evolutionary scale, say no longer an inanimate object or a cold-blooded creature but a warm-blooded animal. Then, when the cycle repeats at a later phase of life, the imagery may appear in human form, and so on. This is not a linear process; it is a cycle that we go through again and again at each major transition point in our life.

Next

I would like to step back for a moment. There are four basic models of transformation which Jung has articulated in his exploration of our inner psychological processes. (1) We saw the role of the ego in "releasing" the guidance of the unconscious in *Symbols of Transformation*, Jung's narrative circulating around the hero myth. Things got more complicated in the two chapters from *Mysterium Coniunctionis*. We noted the alchemical theme of (2) carrying the conflict of opposites until, through the conscientious facing of our inner polarity, a synthesis emerges in time which leads and guides us forward into our destiny, breadth, and depth. In *Mysterium* we were also introduced to the Gnostic theme of (3) withdrawing projections, or, in other words, of extracting the guidance for our life from *within* messy emotional, sometimes physical, situations that we are beset with. This chapter on *Aion* has returned to the two paradigms we found first in *Mysterium* (synthesis of opposites, extraction from onslaught). Jung's efforts here clearly emphasize the Gnostic paradigm of extraction as a means of recovering the true living, guiding spirit. Additionally, *Aion* placed Jung's *psychological efforts in a historical perspective. Aion* also touched on the usefulness of Jung's broad view for therapy. (4) In the next discussion, we will explore Jung's *Answer to Job*. We'll investigate the situation where the Self is out to kill us, where it isn't helping us, where it is trying to destroy us. *Answer to Job* presents the fourth model of the coming to awareness of selfhood as we throw all our resources into the question of what it is to be a genuine person on our genuine path. The "Job" theme, as the fourth paradigm Jung has explored, doesn't appear very often. But where there has been severe psychological and/or physical abuse, it does appear. *Answer to Job* is a very emotionally upsetting work for the reader to digest, but it is a necessary one to digest if we are going to grasp what is at stake at the—often life and death—crossroads that either annihilate or heal. We turn next to the Book of Job.

ANSWER TO JOB

Beginnings

Answer to Job is the one book Jung wrote that he was happy with. He would have rewritten all his other books and essays had he had time, except this one.[212] How did Jung come to write *Answer to Job*? In his account, he takes us back to his book *Aion*:

> The most immediate cause of my writing the book is perhaps to be found in certain problems discussed in my book *Aion*, especially the problems of Christ as a symbolic figure and of the antagonism Christ-Antichrist, represented in the traditional zodiacal symbolism of the two fishes.[213]

Recall Jung's view in *Aion* presents a historical and psychological analysis of the last 2000 years of Western history. He held that there was a first thousand-year phase, marked by the beginning of Christianity, in which the prevailing image of God, Christ, was depicted as light and good and spiritual. That left a hole in the totality of human experience because human nature is not only light and good and spiritual. So, the part of human nature that was not symbolized by the first image of Christ in the first thousand-year period took its revenge, so to speak, in the second thousand-year period and began pressing human experience to move in a direction of worldly exploration. As we saw, there was a first spiritual phase of Western civilization and then a second worldly or material phase of Western civilization. What was also not symbolized in that first image of Christ was the reality of evil, and that split has continued for the 2000 years of Western history. It has been an enduring duality, Christ and the devil, or in Biblical language, Christ and the anti-Christ, in the background of our history.

Jung's commentary on The Book of Job deals with the nature of evil largely excluded from the Christian framework. It addresses the nature of that part of reality that Christianity has marginalized as

---

[212] Marie-Louise von Franz, *C.G. Jung: His Myth in Our Time*, p. 161.
[213] C.G. Jung, *Answer to Job*, The *Collected Works of C.G. Jung*, vol. 11, p. 257; *Answer to Job*, 2010 paperback edition, p. xi.

either the devil (who has to be avoided) or as something with no representation at all in the understanding of God held by significant parts of Christendom. Jung turns back to this problem after raising it in *Aion*. In *Answer to Job*, Jung probes the nature of evil so conveniently swept aside throughout Western history. The contemporary resurgence of evil in the form of renewed fascism around the world, in terms of the naked military aggression currently threatening world stability, and in the terror of nuclear bullying so glibly bandied about by national powers, confirms the horrific closeness of apocalyptic destruction.

There is a personal reference and relevance to the discussion of evil in *Answer to Job*. The book not only has to do with the effect of evil from a broad perspective; it also shows practical relevance to the psychological healing of individuals who, in one way or the other, have experienced evil in their personal lives. What happens to those of us who have been abused, tortured, or have experienced attempted murder, to name a few? Suggestions concerning the healing of that darkness—also receive pride of place in Jung's reflections.

Jung felt the social or historical role of evil, as well as evil's effect on individuals' personal lives, was implied but not totally addressed in *Aion*. *Answer to Job* is an attempt to round out his previous work.

Subjective Emotions

Jung freely admits he wrote *Answer to Job* in a pent-up state of mind:

> I was gripped by the urgency and difficulty of the problem and was unable to throw it off. Therefore I found myself obliged to deal with the whole problem, and I did so in the form of describing a personal experience, carried by subjective emotions.[214]

This book was written out of subjective emotions. Normally, Jung tried to be objective and attentive to empirical rigor in his writing. Here, however, he is wholly subjective. That explains the style of his writing; it is almost a rant. He continues:

---

[214] *Answer to Job*, p. 358; 2010 paperback edition p. xii.

I did so in the form of describing a personal experience, carried by subjective emotions. I deliberately chose this form because I wanted to avoid the impression that I had any idea of announcing an "eternal truth."[215]

He is giving a subjective confession from his experience, as a psychiatrist and a concerned citizen, for all people and peoples in his perimeter who have suffered as the object of evil.

Since I shall be dealing with numinous factors, my feeling is challenged quite as much as my intellect. I cannot, therefore, write in a coolly objective manner, but must allow my emotional subjectivity to speak if I want to describe what I feel when I read certain books of the Bible, or when I remember the impressions I have received from the doctrines of our faith. I do not write as a biblical scholar (which I am not), but as a layman and physician who has been privileged to see deeply into the psychic life of many people. What I am expressing is first of all my own personal view.[216]

I shall not give a cool and carefully considered exegesis that tries to be fair to every detail, but a purely subjective reaction. In this way I hope to act as a voice for many who feel the same way as I do.[217]

Jung wrote *Answer to Job* in a fever. He went to bed with a febrile illness, and later he told Esther Harding that he saw a little imp sitting on his bedpost who dictated the essay to him. When he was finished writing, the fever had abated.[218] That should give us reason to be alert to the style—and to assiduously peer beneath Jung's prose for the psychic reality it is trying to grasp and convey.

Mention must be made of the effect of this work on his readers. In a letter of Jung's to Erich Neumann, Jung says:

---

[215] Ibid.
[216] Ibid., par. 559.
[217] Ibid., par. 561.
[218] Edward Edinger, *Transformation of the God-Image*, pp. 17f.

I could no longer consider the average reader. Rather he has to consider *me*.[219]

Edward Edinger, in his commentary to *Answer to Job*, adds parenthetically:

This is why it is so hard for us to understand *Answer to Job*, you see—because this is the attitude he is writing out of.[220]

Jung continues:

I had to pay this tribute to the pitiless fact of my old age. With the undimmed prospect of all-around incomprehension, I could exercise no suasions and no *captatio benevolentiae* [currying favor]; there was no hope of funneling knowledge into fools.[221]

In his writing *Answer to Job*, he felt it is up to us to meet him more than halfway. In Jung's other works, he did try to meet the reader halfway; here he does not. That puts a burden on the reader, but it is an invitation to our effort I find entirely worthwhile.

The Plan

I will begin by recounting the essence of the Book of Job. Jung's psychological commentary on the biblical account will then occupy us, and we will pay attention to the therapeutic value of Jung's writing for the Jungian analysis of individuals. A look at the wider implications of Jung's point of view, from a cultural and religious perspective, will follow. Throughout, we will see how *Answer to Job* directly touches on the issue of trauma. A "Job" dream will conclude the chapter.

I will be consulting Edward Edinger's *Transformation of the God-Image* (just cited) as we explore Jung's *Answer to Job*. I confess that without Edinger's study guide, I would have little understanding of

---

[219] Ibid., p. 15.
[220] Ibid.
[221] Ibid.

Jung's book. It's a work that seems obscure with respect to its practical applications, but we will recognize it is a highly pertinent one as we unravel Jung's passionate prose. Edinger's writing is an immense aid in this regard.

Summary of the Book of Job

A summary of the Book of Job, and a bird's-eye view of what Jung is going to do with it, will serve us well. Then we will go through the work in more detail.

A rough outline of the Book of Job reads:

> There is a wager in heaven between Satan and Yahweh as to whether or not Job can be turned away from God—kind of a heavenly conspiracy. Satan tells Yahweh that Job worships him, but it is only because his life is going well. Give Job a hard time and you'll see what he is really like. Job is then beset with multiple calamities. Job then questions his situation. "Why is this happening to me?" He calls out to God to explain to him why this is happening, to justify to him the reason for it. He says he is not an evil man, and his life, his behavior does not, in justice, warrant this kind of treatment. Counselors arrive on the scene who tell him, in effect, to quit questioning what is beyond him and just submit and admit that though he may not understand it, God is just. But Job refuses. He perseveres in his questioning and in maintaining his integrity, as he puts it. And then finally, Yahweh manifests. He shows himself in the whirlwind and in his great final speech he says, in effect, "Who are you to question me? Look at all my grandeur." With that Job is silenced and accepts the situation. Yahweh then restores all his property—better than before. That's the bare-bones of the Biblical account.[222]

Jung's commentary, in brief, will begin to orient our understanding. Observe, of course, that Jung's presentation is utter heresy.

Since Yahweh treated Job unjustly and since that fact was registered consciously by Job, the crime that Yahweh committed against Job on account of his unconsciousness required rectification, required an

---

[222] Ibid., p. 28. [slightly modified]

answer. And Jung tells us, in the book, that Yahweh's answer to his unjust treatment of Job was his incarnation as man. Since his encounter with Yahweh, Job, as the image of humanity, had displayed a consciousness superior to Yahweh's, Yahweh was obliged to catch up with him morally, so to speak, and the answer for Yahweh was to become man.[223]

The traditional interpretation holds that the Book of Job shows that God knows better. Up against Yahweh, Job finally capitulates, and the lesson of the book, according to conventional understanding, is "don't question, because God knows better." Jung's response to that, as we'll see—and as we'll be laying this argument out throughout the chapter—is something like this: if you are looking down the barrel of a howitzer, what are you supposed to say? The end of the story is no moral victory for Yahweh; the end of the story exhibits a huge beast beating up a small creature. Job's response was his only choice, and the end of the book's text is not the lesson of the book. The lesson of the book follows in the subsequent books of the Bible where we see the preparation for the birth of Christ. The real meaning of the Book of Job, Jung argues, comes *after* the Book of Job in the subsequent books of the Bible. Job stood up to Yahweh the best he could, and even through his desperation, he *produced a change in Yahweh.* The overall theme of Jung's commentary is the transformation of the God-image—through the courage, as long as he could humanly sustain it, of the person of Job.

That's the biblical side.

The Job Archetype

We turn to Jung's psychological interpretation of the biblical account because we will initially approach the Book of Job as a story with a psychological lesson for us today. Edinger distills Jung's essential understanding so that we have a sense of the big picture to orient us as we dive into the details of Jung's comments. Edinger's distillation

---

[223] Ibid., p. 19.

makes Jung's discussion eminently practical for the process of therapeutic healing.

> Now this story is the prototype of what I call the Job archetype, which pictures a certain typical encounter between ego and the Self.[224]

Here, in an interpretive leap, which forms much of the backbone of Jung's commentary, Yahweh represents that aspect of the Self which we have to deal with under certain circumstances. Those circumstances, as noted, have to do with terrible emotional and physical abuse. Edinger says:

> I distinguish four chief features of the Job archetype. First, there is an encounter between the ego and the greater power.

The psychological core of this book is a concern with the individual experience of being subjected to overwhelming, destructive power. Examples would be rape, child abuse, attempted murder, torture, genocide and so on.

Secondly, there is wounding:

> A wound or a suffering of the ego results from the encounter.

We are attacked, outwardly generally—which produces an emotional or physical (for example, some bodily malady) attack inwardly, and we are emotionally wounded—if not also physically wounded.

Now comes the crucial point, the third point:

> The ego perseveres in insisting upon scrutinizing the experience in search of its meaning. It will not give up in despair or cynicism, but perseveres in the assumption that the experience is meaningful. This corresponds to Jacob's refusal to release the angel that he is wrestling with until he receives a blessing.[225] This ego attitude corresponds to

---

[224] Ibid., p. 29.
[225] Recall the story of Jacob and the angel who broke Jacob's hip [Genesis 32:22-32].

Job's insistence on thinking that he know that his redeemer lives even though he's being mistreated.

The fourth point reads:

As a result of that a divine revelation takes place by which the ego is rewarded with insight into the nature of the transpersonal psyche. And it will be an insight that satisfies the ego. It answers the question in some form or another and brings acceptance.

The most practical relevance of the Job archetype is in this next sentence:

Now this full sequence can take place only if it isn't short circuited by a personalistic or reductive interpretation at step three.[226]

If we say, "I deserved it," or "this is my karma," or "my parental complex set me up for this," we inhibit the subsequent healing manifestation of the Self. Jung is laying out a totally different way of working with psychological experience. Reductive interpretations[227] will kill the healing capacity of psychological experience at this point. That is why it is so dangerous to use a Freudian, i.e., reductive, model with people suffering in the way Job suffered. The archetypal approach, where we don't look at cause, but we question purpose, and we don't stop questioning purpose until we have an answer, allows the Job archetype to evolve. When we don't assume responsibility for the act under which we have innocently suffered, when we *don't take on the guilt*, i.e., feel guilty because of what has *unjustly* happened to us, then the "Job archetype" can evolve. A practical point of our working with the Book of Job is that we learn the clinical attitude necessary to heal suffering caused by the assault of evil. The archetypal approach is such a new point of view, and it flies in the face of our native causal view of life. It can be upsetting to entertain—the point is when *not* to accept guilt.

---

[226] *Transformation of the God-Image*, p. 29. The Job archetype quotes are from p. 29.
[227] Explaining problematic current behavior as a replay of past events. This perspective has its place, but not in Job ordeals.

I will mention one more overview consideration. In addition to examining the story of Job and its psychological relevance for healing the pain when life goes against us as individuals, Jung will also take a wider view and place the insights he gleaned from Job in a larger historical and religious framework. That, in terms of the bare outline, is another aspect of what will follow here.

Victor the Russian

In the spirit of the practical relevance of *Answer to Job* to our psychological journey, I'd like, at this beginning point, to present a Job dream that will be referred to at various points in this chapter.

The dreamer is not a client of mine. He's a client of a colleague who was working with the dreamer about the same time I was conducting a seminar on *Answer to Job*. My colleague called me and said that he had a dream presented to him that he didn't understand. As we worked on the dream, it struck us that it was clearly about Job.

The dreamer worked on the dream with my colleague about 30 years ago, but the dream came about 20 years prior to that. The analysand of my colleague was in therapy with someone else at the time he had the dream. At that time, he was a professor of theology. He subsequently retired and, with his wife, bought a farm.

I see an ancient throne in a dimly lighted but large hallway. On the throne sits one who looks rugged and powerful, whose name (I think) is Victor. When I first see him I say to him, "You are the Russian." [The dream comes from the time of the Cold War.] He gives a laugh which conveys the impression that I have simply stated the obvious. I now learn that in order to survive down through centuries (he has been around about two thousand years), about every hundred years or so he has to find a new reincarnation. This is accomplished by someone, whom Victor selects, drinking a potion which Victor gives him. This person then becomes the new Victor the Russian, a sinister and powerful and dreaded person. A friend of mine (whom I am unable to identify) takes the potion from Victor's hand and tries to give it to me to drink. I refuse it. He tries to force it on me, but I back away, saying I'll never drink it. Some of the potion spills out, and Victor takes the chalice back, saying that it doesn't work anymore anyway. He then drinks it himself. Then the few people there turn to look at me and shrink back. The transition has taken place anyway, in spite of my refusal of the chalice, and my features are apparently turning into those of the Russian. I am so angry that I begin beating on my "friend," who falls to the floor and is powerless to defend himself. He screams, as with both hands I pummel his body in rage. The others do not dare to try to restrain me, but do try to aid my friend. There is a doctor who, between my blows, tries to administer an anesthetic to him. I then cease hitting him, and within myself try to think how the awful power in me could be held in check. I come up with the idea that if the threat of an atomic bomb were held over my head, I would be stopped. The thought itself makes it seem that such is the case, that such an A-bomb is in readiness, and I begin to accept the fact that I must now bear the consequences of 'being' this Victor the Russian. I tie a kind of veil or turban around my head, and arise reluctantly to begin my new life.[228]

We'll come back to the dream. At this point, I encourage you to just let it rumble around in your entrails for a bit. It's a terribly powerful dream that, by the end of the chapter, we will be in a position to let evoke our full and thoughtful response.

Lectori Benevolo and Motto

Consider the Lectori Benevolo[229] at the beginning of *Answer to Job*. The words mean "to the kind reader." Edinger comments:

With this phrase Jung is asking for the indulgence of the reader whom he knows he is about to offend. He is approaching us with elaborate courtesy because he knows he is going to stir up rhinoceros-like affects and as he tells us in another place, rhinoceroses don't like to be surprised, so they should be treated with elaborate courtesy. That is how I understand that particular phrase "to the kind reader." He is asking for our kindness in view of the offence he is about to offer. Because as soon as you begin to look honestly into the material in this book, you realize it is going to offend almost everybody. If you are not offended, you probably don't understand what he is saying. Either one will be offended that God contradicts the familiar God-image that one cherishes in one's own religious confession or formulation. Either that or if one is a secular

---

[228] The verbatim text is courtesy of the dreamer.
[229] *Answer to Job*, par. 553.

rationalist he will be offended that Jung takes so seriously the primitive, anthropomorphic God-image that rationalists have long since discredited. One or the other stand point is going to be offended and it is quite possible that a single person will be offended at both levels at the same time. *So I urge all of you to admit it, "you're annoyed."*[230]

The epigram or motto: "I am distressed for thee, my brother … ." is richly instructive. Edinger's comments are of paramount importance:

In the German original of *Answer to Job* this motto appears in the Latin of the Vulgate—*Doleo super te frater mi* . . . The meaning of these words is not accurately conveyed by the Authorized Version passage that appears in the English translation. The actual translation should read "I grieve for you my brother," because he is grieving over a brother's death. This isn't just a matter of being distressed—the word *doleo* means I grieve, I suffer a loss.

The background of this quotation is highly significant. It is an utterance of David's concerning his dear friend Jonathan. Jonathan, the son of King Saul, had just died in a battle with the Philistines, along with his father.[231]

So, there is Saul and Jonathan on the one hand, and there is David on the other.

They [Saul and Jonathan] had both perished in the same battle. And David is singing an elegy to them in which these lines appear, "Oh, Jonathan, in your death I am stricken, I grieve for you Jonathan, my brother."[232]

You have to remember that this motto is directed at the "kind reader," namely at us—we who are reading it. And Jung is saying "I grieve for you my brother who is about to read this work."

Let's spend a few moments examining the Biblical context of these words: Saul was the *first* king of Israel, and although the spirit of Yahweh was with him at the outset, it turned negative and destroyed him.

---

[230] *Transformation of the God-Image*, p. 23. [emphasis added]
[231] Ibid., p. 24.
[232] 2 Samuel 1:26, Jerusalem Bible (modified).

David was the *second* king of Israel, and the spirit of Yahweh which had abandoned Saul entered David, who then had a successful reign.

Now Jonathan was the son of Saul, but he was a loyal friend of David, though David was destined to replace Saul as the king's successor. Remember that Jonathan was his beloved, loyal friend. You see, this was a moment of momentous transition between the reign of King Saul and that of King David.

. . .

And Jonathan, the son of Saul, is caught between conflicting loyalties. Loyalty as his father's son on the one hand, and to the King-to-be, David, on the other hand. But he was not able to choose wholeheartedly for David. If he had he would have gone over to David's party and would not have been with his father during battle with the Philistines and died with him. His residual dependence on the outworn state of being is what killed him.[233]

The figures play out the dynamics of a shift in value systems. Saul is Jonathan's father, but Jonathan is David's friend. Saul is the old king, which means the old values, and David is the new king, which means the new values in a period of cultural transition. Jonathan is attached to the old values, and that is what kills him. If he had been able to attach himself to the new values, he would have survived. And it's that death that Jung says he is grieving for. He is grieving for us who are like Jonathan, who can't realize we are in a period of cultural and religious transition and are stuck in the old value system. Jung must have been thinking something like, "I have been working hard for the last forty years to introduce a new value system. Now at the age of 77, all I can say is, 'I feel sorry for you if you can't follow me.'"

I refer back to *Aion* for a brief retrospect. Recall Jung feels we are in a fundamental shift in religious and cultural values moving from the twentieth to the twenty-first century. He is trying to communicate a new understanding of religion and culture, and here, in his fever, he feels sorry for people who can't follow the new. What is the main shift in values? As seen in *Aion*, the shift in values has to do with no

---

[233] *Transformation of the God-Image*, pp. 24f.

longer projecting the Self onto a religious figure, an institution, or even another person but to begin seeing the Self as an inner content, with all the ramifications of that statement introduced in *Aion*.

Edinger clarifies the importance of the preceding discussion:

> I am going into all of this because it is relevant to the way Jung perceives those who are about to read his book. It corresponds to Jung's feeling of the contemporary world to whom he is sending this book. You see, like David, he was all alone. About seven months before he died he unburdened himself in a letter to a person who had sent him a book, someone he didn't know. Here are some of the things he had to say.[234]

> I had to understand I was unable to make the people see what I am after. I am practically alone. There are a few who understand this and that, but almost nobody sees the whole. . . . I have failed in my foremost task to open people's eyes to the fact that man has a soul and there is a buried treasure in the field and that our religion and philosophy is in a lamentable state.[235]

Edinger continues:

> *Answer to Job* is written out of that kind of lonely awareness.[236]

Evolution of the God-Image

The first sentence of the body of *Answer to Job* reads:

> The Book of Job is a landmark in the long historical development of a divine drama.[237]

Jung's view holds that one of the threads discernible through history is people's changing perceptions of what God is. In our Western, Christian-stamped civilization, we have gone from the matriarchy to the gods of Greece to Yahweh and to the Christian portrayal of God

---

[234] Ibid., p. 25.
[235] Ibid.
[236] Ibid.
[237] *Answer to Job*, par. 560.

and Jesus. Now, Jung feels, we are at a point where a new understanding of that image of God is imperative if we are to survive. How is that going to occur? He feels it is going to occur within individuals. These individuals are those who have been the object of the dark side of God, namely the object of evil events which provoke an overpowering assault of dark and negative emotions. The victims seeking sanity have to struggle with the imagery that is activated in and through their experience of the horror. As they are able to work with their emotions in the sense of this Job paradigm, they will be involved in transforming that violent image of God, which has been neglected throughout Western history, into a more humane image of God that fits into the totality of what we can possibly envision God to be. Now is the period of history when the image of God will be relieved of its one-sidedness and reformed into a balanced mixture of opposites. What has been acknowledged by the Christian religion up to now has only been a "light" God. What was seen in the Old Testament was an *unconscious* mixture of light and dark. Now the challenge is to bring the dark and the light into a conscious understanding of what a transformed image of God is.

It appears we are dealing with a paradox. I just observed we need a cultural shift in our understanding of God, and now I put the focus of that change in the image of God on the individual. That apparent paradox is resolved when we understand the role of the individual in the cultural shift. In this period of history, the challenge presented to the individual is to work on their version of this transition of the God-image. In time, in the long run, it is just possible that these individual efforts will coalesce into a larger movement of a general reevaluation of what God is. Each individual who wrestles with a Job experience will be coming up with a new transformed image of God in themselves. It's Jung's hope that if enough people continue to do this individually, there will be a general shift with the individual efforts merging into a larger movement of the reevaluation of the nature of God.

In helping restore the integrity of our religious life, we can find our version of this transformation, one by one. I believe Jung would say if there is a chance for the world's survival, a new religious awakening will have to occur out of the kind of individual experience we are looking at in *Answer to Job*.

This is what Jung means by "divine drama"—the evolution of our understanding of God over the course of our civilization's history. As he anticipates it, the impetus for this evolution will start with a deeper religious experience on the part of those individuals so touched by the Job problem and dynamic, as I mentioned. In addition to helping us to work with trauma, the purpose of *Answer to Job* is to show us how we might participate in a religious renewal in our time—contributing our little part to the sweep of historical change.[238]

Wound and Weapon

We need to scrutinize and digest the following sentence. It informs Jung's psychological approach and is hardly intuitively obvious.

> And just as there is a secret tie between the wound and the weapon, so the affect corresponds to the violence of the deed that caused it.[239]

I'll explicate that by analogy. Since we are dealing with the effects of violence, my analogy will have to be gruesome. I apologize. Let's suppose a person is attacked by somebody with a branding iron. Or let's suppose a person was clubbed by somebody with a certain size club. The mark that the branding iron or the club leaves on the victim's body will be determined by the shape of the branding iron or the club.

If the victim wanted to confirm who the criminal was, that person would compare the image left in their flesh with the object in the possession of the criminal who could have inflicted the wound. Obviously, the situation is not that simple, but I give examples to make the point that the shape of a physical injury has something of the shape of the injuring weapon about it. That is the basis of Jung's

---

[238] Jung was not naive about how arduous the sweep would be, predicting it might take about 600 years. Edward Edinger, *Archetype of the Apocalypse*, p. 33.
[239] *Answer to Job*, par. 561.

psychology embedded in *Answer to Job*. The physical wounding just noted was, of course, an analogy for emotional wounding. Jung's grounding point, then, is that the dream or fantasy images by which our psyche responds to a trauma are an indicator of the source of the trauma, of where that trauma came from. The images that our psyches generate to symbolize the emotions that emerge as we endure the pain of a life trauma are an indication of the factor that caused the trauma. By looking at the images that represent our emotional response to the trauma, at the images that occur in dreams and fantasies following the trauma, we get some indication of the cause of the trauma.

This is the unexpected and fundamentally disagreeable part of Jung's observation and position in this matter: *The image that the psyche uses to express the agent causing the trauma is often an image of God.* If therapeutic efforts at healing the trauma continue at a sufficiently deep level, in time, dreams turn to express that it is God who has caused their trauma—the dark and destructive side of God—the aspect of God that contemporary religious consciousness refuses to admit exists. This will become clearer when we return to the dream of Victor the Russian.

This is such an offensive idea to normative thinking; I will linger here a moment. As just noted, because we see in the dreams of people who have been seriously abused that it is God who is abusing them, Jung then suggests that what we are looking at in these people is an image of the dark side of the prevailing, ruling God. That is what is causing their wound.

Society has a particular image of God at its spiritual foundation, and for us, that image of God is a God that is good. This completely ignores the part of God that is evil. That means that the ignored part of the human experience, symbolized by the dark and destructive side of God, operates outside of the view of consciousness. It is there, and it is operative. It is just not seen, acknowledged, and symbolized.

The people who perpetrate crimes on other individuals—because that is what this is about, practically, it's about those individuals who have endured criminal behavior enacted on them—the criminals are acting

155

out that part of life which does not have official recognition. They are acting out the reality denied existence in the prevailing image of God. The people who are injured are thus injured by the collective shadow, which is another way of saying this.

Jung's idea—and now I return to the first sentence of the book concerning the "divine drama"—is that if the socially accepted values can begin to shift, perhaps human behavior will begin to shift. The person who is living out evil on somebody else is acting out of that part of the psyche not symbolized by societal norms as part of God. When we look at the dreams that occur in these perpetrators and their victims, the behavior is carried out by the side of God not recognized in the prevailing religious canon.

The point is so central it deserves our continuing attention. The socially omnipresent image of God is what determines social values and what determines the emotions and impulses that are allowed to pass through the contemporary filters of accepted experience. All those aspects of human nature that are excluded from consideration and recognition by the collective value system are what, in fact, create the tragic behaviors of a given era. Victims of evil have been the object of violence denied as belonging to the full nature of God.

That way of conceptualizing the wounder and the wounded takes some getting used to. Put in the most basic terms, victims suffer an onslaught of the part of the image of God that needs to be recognized. This is a fundamental position of Jung's. This is how he links the dark side of God to individuals' suffering, to those individuals who have dark God imagery present in the psyche.

Grasping why Jung makes so much of the dark side of the God-image in certain people is crucial. Building on this understanding, we will accordingly explore how we can heal this situation. But before a full grasp of healing can occur, a full grasp of the complexity of wounding must precede it. Another look at Jung's phrasing will bring the discussion back to his formulation in *Answer to Job*.

The "secret tie between the wound and the weapon," between the God-image in society and its presence in individuals who have been abused, is Jung's way of saying that the unknown aspect of the God-image is at the back of certain types of human misery. The abuse may have been enacted on an individual by another individual, but, as noted, the way the dreams at times symbolize the abuse is that the abuse is being carried out by the God image.

"So the affect corresponds to the violence of the deed that caused it."[240] The affect would be the rage that follows victimhood, and the way that rage is symbolized is as the dark side of God. The dark side of God is the mirror image of what caused the injury. The dark side of God is perpetrated through an individual, but the energy that is visited upon the victim through the individual perpetrator is symbolized by the dark side of God.

Amorality and Integrity

In response to Yahweh's tirade against Job, Job answers Yahweh:

> Behold, I am of small account; what shall I answer thee?
> I lay my hand on my mouth.
> I have spoken once, and I will not answer;
> twice, but I will proceed no further.[241]

This is traditionally interpreted as Job recanting his position.[242]

To those who claim that God is right and Job is wrong, Jung replies that the opinion that God is just is erroneous and is based on God's power. Power seduces the naive person into believing that because something is dominant, it is right. It's a version of "might makes right." That is hardly justice. The comforter[243] says: "Is it fit to say

---

[240] Ibid., par. 561.
[241] Ibid., par. 564, Job 40:3-5, Revised Standard Version.
[242] Ibid., par. 566.
[243] The term for those figures in the Book of Job who take Yahweh's side, telling Job to be accept with equanimity what is happening because God is right.

157

to a king, Thou art wicked? And to princes to claim: Ye are ungodly?"[244] An authority figure is seen as just because they are powerful. Likewise, this is tantamount to equating power with goodness. If something is big, it is right. That destructive error appears to be universal. It is worth parenthetically noting that this is one of the shifts our time is demanding we make. The nuclear age has made it catastrophically suicidal to ignore the wanton capriciousness of power.

This can be extrapolated to social dimensions. We have one standard for judging the acts of an individual, but if a corporation does something, a different standard is applied. If an individual is unjust, it is not okay. If a corporation is unjust, it is okay. If Indianapolis wins the Superbowl, we are a good town. If we lose, we are not a good town. Jung is laying out the background of every decision we make. Power is good. Stronger is better. Biggest is best.

Jung now is challenging the view of comforters, which he feels is so typical of general thinking: when something bad happens to you, you deserve it. Or if somebody bigger than you, or if a bigger group, or if a large group does something harmful, it's okay. The voice of the individual is snuffed out. Jung is challenging Yahweh with these words:

> If Yahweh, as we would expect of a sensible human being, were really conscious of himself, he would, in view of the true facts of the case, at least have put an end to the panegyrics on his justice. But he is too unconscious to be moral.[245]

This is effectively Job's message to Yahweh, Jung feels.

> Morality presupposes consciousness. By this I do not mean to say that Yahweh is imperfect or evil, like a gnostic demiurge. He is everything in its totality; therefore, among other things, he is total justice, and also its total opposite. At least this is the way he must be conceived if one is to form a unified picture of his character. We must only remember that

---

[244] Job 34:18 Authorized Version.
[245] *Answer to Job*, par. 574.

what we have sketched is no more than an anthropomorphic picture which is not even particularly easy to visualize. From the way the divine nature expresses itself we can see that the individual qualities are not adequately related to one another, with the result that they fall apart into mutually contradictory acts. For instance, Yahweh regrets having created human beings, although in his omniscience he must have known all along what would happen to them.[246]

When a person has been the victim of power, the temptation is to take on the point of view of the power that has victimized the person. In psychoanalysis, this is called "identification with the aggressor."[247] A related term for it is the "Stockholm syndrome."[248] That is what concerns Jung here. Because Yahweh is powerful, the temptation when we are an innocent victim of abusive situations is to disidentify with our own values and value and take on both from the person who is hurting us. Hands have been laid on a person, and the temptation is for that person to treat others from the perspective of those who have meted out the harm.

Here is an example.

I was working with a woman who had been raped. I started working with her after she had reported the incident to the police. She had been seeing a female therapist for a while, and then she wanted to do some dream work. The female therapist had taken her to the police station. The first thing the cop said was, "What did you do to provoke the guy?" If it's big and powerful and you are the victim, there is something wrong. Jung is saying that way of looking at

---

[246] Ibid.

[247] "A defence mechanism that indicates taking the role of the aggressor and his functional attributes, or imitating his aggressive and behavioral modality, when a psychological trauma brings about the hopeless dilemma of being either a victim or an abuser."
https://en.wikipedia.org/wiki/Identification_with_the_Aggressor.

[248] "A condition in which hostages develop a psychological bond with their captors during captivity. It results from a rather specific set of circumstances, namely the power imbalances contained in hostage-taking, kidnapping, and abusive relationships."
https://en.wikipedia.org/wiki/Stockholm_syndrome.

accountability is a cultural attitude—based right in our view of God. Job's victimization is interpreted by mainstream theology in the certainty that Job had done something to provoke Yahweh. The first thing to know when working with a victim is to get them out of the self-blaming way of thinking; otherwise, the healing process will never establish. We are taking this distortion of blame a step further and looking at the cultural ramifications of where "blaming the victim" comes from and how the behavior of individuals living in such a culture supports the blaming.[249]

Job Sees Yahweh

What are we going to do about these travesties of Justice? Jung's text turns to this question.

> Yahweh abandons his faithful servant to the evil spirit and lets him fall without compunction or pity into the abyss of physical and moral suffering. From the human point of view Yahweh's behaviour is so revolting that one has to ask oneself whether there is not a deeper motive hidden behind it. Has Yahweh some secret resistance against Job? … What does man possess that God does not have? Because of his littleness, puniness, and defencelessness against the Almighty, he possesses, as we have already suggested, a somewhat keener consciousness based on self-reflection: he must, in order to survive, always be mindful of his impotence. God has no need of this circumspection, for nowhere does he come up against an insuperable obstacle that would force him to hesitate and hence make him reflect on himself.[250]

The healing of victimization, on the individual level, is that the individual begins to hold to his innocence and not let his consciousness be snuffed out by the power of the perpetrator or by the collective thinking that colludes with the perpetrator in saying

---

[249] Jung is investigating the attitude that often underlies and maintains the persistence of traumatic pain and damage. There is also much to be learned from Bessel van der Kolk's *The Body Keeps the Score: Brain, Mind, and Body in the Healing of Trauma*—a work of remarkably clear insight and deeply compelling feeling.

[250] *Answer to Job*, par. 579.

that there is nothing wrong with the perpetrator's behavior. We have to say loud and clear we have been victimized and that we are innocent.

We will now look at the case of victimhood through the lens of the Job archetype and seek from where healing can come.

How can we understand trauma archetypally? Edinger gives us a very helpful commentary. His comment refers our discussion to the practical value of *Answer to Job*.

> Now these passages bring up a fundamental question that I want you to reflect on: In dealing with psychic problems in ourselves and in our patients, when is it proper to use a personalistic approach and when is it proper to use an archetypal approach?[251]

When do the considerations that we are entertaining apply to the practice of Jungian therapy, and when do they not apply? In other words, when is the Job archetype truly constellated, and when can that symbolism be properly applied? When should we proceed reductively? And when should we proceed archetypally? When do we say to somebody, "You don't deserve this. You must not take personal responsibility for this. This was unjust. As I understand healing, your job is to maintain innocence. Our job is to work with your dreams to see how they begin to resolve this." That would be the "Job archetype" way. The other way would be to say, "How did you set yourself up for this?" Both of these alternatives, under certain circumstances, are valid. I am clarifying what we have been discussing, and I am placing that in the overall context of the enterprise of therapy.

It is a lot easier to make this distinction theoretically than practically. Sometimes it is easier to see how an individual has set themselves up for the upset. I can confess that the destructive things that have happened to me in my life, I have inflicted upon myself. When I can see I have done something stupid to cause my own demise, and I do need to take personal responsibility for my actions, it would be

---

[251] *Transformation of the God-Image*, p. 31.

fallacious to think about my actions from the archetypal perspective. Taking an archetypal stance would simply allow me to slip out of my own personal responsibility for my actions. But when someone is a true victim or is a victim far beyond any proportion of what they might have said or done to activate a tragedy, then the situation is different. It's a very delicate question in our work: How much responsibility should an individual take? We can take too much responsibility, or we can take too little. Part of the art of Jungian analysis is feeling: Do we proceed reductively here? Or does the therapist say, "this is not your fault." Certainly, with children, we can see the wisdom of the archetypal approach. Or if we are working with adults and are discussing the traumas they have sustained in childhood, the archetypal approach is appropriate. We have to carefully assess the events in an adult's life.

Here's an example. A big-shot Jungian colleague got caught sleeping with his analysands—several of his analysands. He attended a professional seminar, also attended by a friend of mine, where he was bemoaning his fate as Job. His colleagues, my friend reported, sat around the table saying some version of "Oh, you poor man." I responded vociferously to my conversation partner that the acts of the big-shot analyst were simply immoral and hurtful. When a man like him violates trust, he needs to hear that, "You deserve the trouble you have brought on yourself." There were, understandably, professional consequences.

The Background of Events

We have taken account of Job as the victim. We have talked about the Job archetype and a few first remarks about healing. The question of healing will further occupy our attention.

Jung picks up the discussion.

> Why Job's torments and the divine wager should suddenly come to an end is not quite clear. So long as Job does not actually die, the pointless

162

suffering could be continued indefinitely. We must, however, keep an eye on the background of all these events:[252]
Now comes another very important sentence:

> It is just possible that *something in this background* will gradually begin to take shape as a compensation for Job's undeserved suffering ... .[253]

So, if the ego can maintain its integrity in the face of injustice, justice is constellated from within the unconscious—if the ego does not falsely take responsibility for what happened.

Edinger's summing up is priceless.

> What that means is that injustice, especially if it is consciously perceived, constellates its correction in the other—in the unconscious or in the outside world. In other words, *injustice consciously perceived and borne constellates justice.*[254]

The healing of the attack by evil, then, is threefold: the recognition of injustice, holding innocence against blame, turning inside and watching the development that starts from within as a result. That is what makes the unconscious creative when injustice has overruled sanity—or that is what allows the unconscious to become creative—when injustice is perceived, critiqued, and borne. There, the ego is a servant of that process.

When the Job archetype is activated, the stream of development starts in the recognition of horror and then holding onto integrity through despair. It's not that we don't feel miserable. We do feel miserable. But we don't give up and say, "life is meaningless." Even though all facts speak to the contrary, that life is one big cesspool, that life is absurd, the ego maintains a different attitude. That is why Jung will not shy away from the importance of faith.

---

[252] *Answer to Job*, par. 583.
[253] Ibid. [emphasis added]
[254] *Transformation of the God-Image*, p. 17.

We call on all our effort not to surrender to cynicism even though we see no meaning in the horror. As therapists, we have to support that position—usually against a terrible and raging emotional storm. All we can say is "I don't know." But we can follow that with, "Do not stop asking the question until we do know." The ego maintaining such an attitude is what allows the unconscious to become creative. The challenge is to hold steady in the despair.

Previously, we investigated the wound and the wounder. Now, take clear note of how important it is that healing is a non-ego process. One of Jung's purposes in *Answer to Job* is to lay bare how we can heal.

This, to recall the beginning of *Answer to Job,* is the shift to another level of consciousness, described as the "David" level of consciousness. Here Jung's gift is tremendous. How do we heal from tragedy?

A Dialectic in God

What does Jung mean by a dialectic in God? Jung is speaking about Yahweh:

> Altogether, he pays so little attention to Job's real situation that one suspects him of having an ulterior motive which is more important to him:[255]

Now comes the important sentence:

> Job is no more than the outward occasion for an inward process of dialectic in God.

In the unconscious, there is a process to make our knowledge of ourselves complete. Put differently, but to the same effect, in the Self there is a process to make our knowledge of the Self complete. The ego of individuals who stand firm against the onslaught of injustice has activated the inner process which aims at completion. That is the

---

[255] *Answer to Job*, par. 587.

dialectic to reshape and reform the depth and breadth of the inner Self. And since the Self is often symbolized by images of God, Jung refers to the "inward process of dialectic" as a process going on in the image of God. The Self, symbolized by images of God, initiates a process within itself to transform. This transformed Self and its frequent representation in these God-images is the foundation of a new personality of strength and conviction that begins to heal the damage done by the trauma. Despair gives way to the path of a richer and fuller life as its bedrock is slowly but increasingly strengthened within.

Articulating the religious implications of this, Jung writes:

> The new factor is something that has never occurred before in the history of the world, the unheard-of fact that, without knowing it or wanting it, a mortal man is raised by his moral behaviour above the stars in heaven, from which position of advantage he can behold the back of Yahweh, the abysmal world of "shards."[256]

In other words, the human ego is now in a position to be more conscious than the representation of God, or if we use the psychological language, the Self. That is the turning moment: we don't feel ourselves as a child against a parent who knows better. We raise our own capacity for discrimination to be equal to those dark events in our lives.

> Nevertheless, Job got his satisfaction, without Yahweh's intending it and possibly without himself knowing it, as the poet would have it appear. Yahweh's allocutions have the unthinking yet none the less transparent purpose of showing Job the brutal power of the demiurge: "This is I, the creator of all the ungovernable, ruthless forces of Nature, which are not subject to any ethical laws. I, too, am an amoral force of Nature, a purely phenomenal personality that cannot see its own back."[257]

That is what we need to see about our understanding of God. In fact, the Western image of God is not merely a God of love but also a God

---

[256] *Answer to Job*, par. 595.
[257] Ibid., par. 605.

of power and dominance. That is our highest value, not in word, but in deed.

Consciousness of ultimate things follows from healing:

> This is, or at any rate could be, a moral satisfaction of the first order for Job, because through this declaration man, in spite of his impotence, is set up as a judge over God himself.[258]

Edinger discusses the point in terms of the container and the contained. It's yet another way of visualizing the shift between the first and second kings that began this chapter. In the first system, the ego is contained in God. We say, therefore, "God knows better. God's will gives me comfort. I follow God's will, and that justifies my life." That is the ego being contained in God. But with Job, there's a shift. The ego is the container for God. It no longer simply defers judgment. It judges. It no longer simply feels protected. It questions. We could say that when there is a shift of container and contained, we are moving from a child/parent relationship to an adult/adult God relationship.

Sophia and the Transformation of God

That is the basic psychological argument. A quick review is in order. The attack by evil, in order to be healed, demands the maintaining of innocence and truthfulness in the face of the temptation to feel guilty. It requires living in the despair of knowing the attack is unjust and not having an answer—until the unconscious begins to produce a way out, which would be a new awareness of the Self and, I believe, at the same time, a new outer opportunity for development. The images symbolizing the Self are frequently images of God. The transformation of the Self in the interiority of individuals are small instances of a larger transformation of a culture's understanding and portrayal of God. On a historical level, we have seen such a transformation in our inquiry into Job, and it is desperately needed. God as power is at a dead end. It will kill us. The nuclear question means there is no longer room for the smallest measure of error.

---

[258] Ibid., par. 606.

Now Jung shifts from a discussion of the psychological argument he extracts from the Book of Job to the implications of what he has just presented.

Jung's next commentary turns away from the Book of Job. He interprets the *place* of the Book of Job within the order of the other books of the Bible. He sees psychological relevance here because he takes the order of the books of the Bible psychologically. This drives Biblical scholars crazy. As you probably know, the order of the books of the Bible doesn't necessarily have to do with the dates that they were written in Hebrew history. The Bible is a compilation. Jung's feeling is that the way the Bible is arranged, regardless of the historical order, is itself a reflection of a psychological pattern. *He now turns to look at the books in the Bible that come after the Book of Job to represent the psychology that is likely to transpire after a Job event.*

To pursue Jung's exposition, I draw on Edinger's overview of the books of the Bible in his *Bible and the Psyche.*[259]

Traditionally the Hebrew Bible is divided into three major genres of books. First is the historical books, starting with Genesis, Exodus, and so on—those books are all about the history of Israel. The next section is called the poetical/wisdom books, and that section begins with Job, Psalms, Proverbs, Ecclesiastes, and the Song of Solomon. There are also some apocryphal books in there. The last section is the prophets: Isaiah, Jeremiah, and so on. With the beginning of Psalms and Proverbs, a new figure appears in the Bible: Wisdom or Sophia (Sophia is the Greek for Wisdom). Jung claims that is no accident. Wisdom/Sophia is the representation of the feminine that Yahweh needs to incarnate himself in Christ. That it is putting it in the Biblical language. To put it in psychological language, the feminine is what is generated when we consciously face the evil which has been visited upon us. That is how the feminine is generated. The response of the psyche to our carrying this darkness is the generation of Wisdom.

---

[259] Edward Edinger, *The Bible and the Psyche*, pp. 12f.

Let's look at Jung's view on that. He gives some examples of Wisdom (I'll refer to her by her Greek name, Sophia):

We hear about Sophia in Proverbs 8 in this context. It's a second creation myth—second to the one in Genesis. Sophia is speaking.

> The Lord possessed me in the beginning of his way,
> before his works of old.
> I was set up from everlasting, from the beginning,
> or ever the earth was.
> When there were no depths, I was brought forth;
> when there were no fountains abounding with water.
> . . . .
> When he established the heavens, I was there
> , ...
> when he marked out the foundations of the earth,
> then I was by him, as a master workman,
> and I was daily his delight … .[260]

In this account of the creation, Sophia exists before the birth of the world. That is what Jung bases his next discussion on—the birth of the feminine after the crisis of evil and the subsequent containment of darkness. The response of Sophia to the injustice in the Book of Job is a foundational act evoking what makes the transformation of Yahweh possible.

Jung, reflecting on how and to what purpose Sophia appears in the Bible after the Book of Job, puts it like this:

> [Yahweh] has remembered a feminine being who is no less agreeable to him than to man, a friend and playmate from the beginning of the world, the first-born of all God's creatures, a stainless reflection of his glory and a master workman. … There must be some dire necessity responsible for this anamnesis of Sophia: things simply could not go on as before, the "just" God could not go on committing injustices, and the "Omniscient" could not behave any longer like a clueless and thoughtless human being. Self-reflection becomes an imperative

---

[260] *Answer to Job*, pars. 609f., citing Proverbs 8:22–24 (Authorized Version); 27, 29–31 (Authorized Version, modified).

necessity, and for this Wisdom is needed. Yahweh has to remember his absolute knowledge; for, if Job gains knowledge of God, then God must also learn to know himself. It just could not be that Yahweh's dual nature should become public property and remain hidden from himself alone. Whoever knows God has an effect on him. The failure of the attempt to corrupt Job has changed Yahweh's nature.[261]

The biblical account of the appearance of Sophia after the Book of Job is the response from the depths to the consciously endured despair and the conviction of the innocence of the unjustly attacked victim. The arrangement of the books of the Bible symbolizes this process. Sophia is the appearance of the capacity for justice out of an endured condition of injustice.

Edinger succinctly calls these words the most important sentence in the book.[262]

Whoever knows God has an effect on him.[263]

Regeneration and healing have begun.

Yahweh must become man precisely because he has done man a wrong. ... Because his creature has surpassed him he must regenerate himself.[264]

As a psychiatrist, Jung is concerned with this regeneration of our interior experience. The previous attacking images of the Self soften with the appearance of Sophia. Additionally, Jung feels that what we can observe happening in the individual in terms of the restitution to justice of central values is the manifestation of a change that could, in time, become a broader and social one. I touched on this a moment ago. The way for a culture to evolve, Jung holds, is for individuals in that culture to begin evolving. It's up to the individual to initiate broader change. It's a hopeful viewpoint. The individuals' struggle with despair at the injustice that nearly massacred them in the way

---

[261] Ibid., par. 617.
[262] *Transformation of the God-Image*, p. 61.
[263] *Answer to Job*, par. 617.
[264] Ibid., par. 640.

Jung has conceived it in *Answer to Job* could be, in the microcosm, the beginning of a religious transformation of the society's central values and understanding of God in the macrocosm. It's Jung's hope that the dynamics of healing he has uncovered through his reflections on evil and the Book of Job would start in individuals and then would spread to the wider society. Historical change, he felt, always begins with somebody and somebodies.[265]

In terms of our earlier scrutiny, the new shift is the shift from contained to container. We don't throw out religion, but we see it as what we contain, not what contains us.

Next, we'll focus on what I might call Jung's "theology"—or at least the further implications of his position for our religious life.

The Opposites Possess

He begins:

> The fact that Christian ethics leads to collisions of duty speaks in its favour. By engendering insoluble conflicts and consequently an *afflictio animae*, [affliction of the soul] it brings man nearer to a knowledge of God. All opposites are of God, therefore man must bend to this burden; and in so doing he finds that God in his "oppositeness" has taken possession of him, incarnated himself in him. He becomes a vessel filled with divine conflict.[266]

What will be the main constituent of a new religious attitude, Jung asks? What will religious people be doing 200 years from now? Or,

---

[265] Recall we considered the link between the Self and images of God in the last chapter, primarily in an inner sense, i.e., that the Self is not infrequently symbolized by images of God—that's just the way we are made. In the previous chapter, we likewise considered that the effect of our working on the unity and truth of the Self appears in dreams as renewed images of God. That the renewal of the image of God in the individual may be the first step in the renewal of religious experience of God on a societal and historical level is a viewpoint that remains dear to Jung through to the end of his life.
[266] Ibid., par. 659.

200 years from now, how should humanity understand what the religious is? His answer is "suffering conflict." That is the religious task. Not being good. Not fulfilling all the righteous definitions we have imposed. The individual who endures their experience of injustice and carries it, knowing that it is not just a meaningless accident—that is a religious experience. Jung is unofficially redefining religious experience. I carry the opposites of the cross inside myself. Jesus does not do it for me. The nature of God is a polarity. And when we are torn by polarity, we are conscious of God. This is not simply a matter of following our bliss or making chicken soup or seven habits of highly effective Jungians. It is allowing ourselves to be caught up in life to the point where this conflict sits in the center of our soul.

As noted, we've covered the basic argument; now, we are looking at the implications or ramifications of the discussion. An important sentence, as far as ramifications go, follows:

> Because the *imago Dei* [the image of God] pervades the whole human sphere and makes mankind its involuntary exponent,[267]

That's another important phrase "makes mankind its voluntary exponent."

> It is just possible that the four-hundred year-old schism in the Church and the present division of the political world into two hostile camps are both expressions of the unrecognized polarity of the dominant archetype.[268]

Freud placed sexuality as the instinct that drives all life. Adler said the power drive was the most important factor in psychological motivation. Other schools of psychology have other ideas. Jung puts the unfolding of the Self as the most powerful dynamic in the personality. We are too often unaware of the opposites within that make up the unconscious Self. When that is the case, we unknowingly live out the inner opposites as polarity, conflict, schism,

---

[267] Ibid., par. 660.
[268] Ibid.

and hostility with destructive results for ourselves and others. That is what is behind the fractured mess of our time.

Edinger puts it in a matter-of-fact way:

The basic axiom here is that the *"imago Dei* [image of God] pervades the whole human sphere and makes mankind its involuntary exponent." I prefer a slightly different translation of that sentence (which hinges on how you translate the verb *darstellen*): "The *imago Dei* pervades the whole human sphere and is involuntarily represented by mankind."

Our behaviors represent the split within the God-image.

The God image (*imago Dei*), therefore, as the core archetype of the collective unconscious, is the central agent and creative authority which determines the functioning of all individuals and all organic groupings of individuals. [He follows, as just mentioned, the movement from the individual to the society.] And by organic groupings I mean all families, tribes, factions, parties, religions, nations—all groupings small or large which are unified by mutual identification with an origin, a cause, or a creed. These origins, causes and creed will be expressions of the God-image which is the operative central agent in the psyche of that particular group. What that means then is that in all conflicts between nations, creeds—different factions of all kinds, each side will be acting out a commitment to its own version of the God-image. In other words, the conflict between any two factions is a conflict within the God-image itself.

. . .

This is my effort to elaborate what is condensed in this one sentence, "The *imago Dei* pervades the whole human sphere and it is involuntarily represented by mankind." As that becomes visible to you, it changes your whole understanding of the functioning of the collective psyche of humanity—of the way it manifests itself politically, and religiously, and factionally in all its various aspects.[269]

---

[269] The previous four quote are from *Transformation of the God-Image*, p. 81.

Continuing Incarnation

Now Jung discusses his grasp of a fuller religious life.

> This Spirit of Truth and Wisdom is the Holy Ghost by whom Christ was begotten. He is the spirit of physical and spiritual procreation ... . Since he is the Third Person of the Deity, this is as much as to say that God will be begotten in creaturely man. This implies a tremendous change in man's status ... .[270]

And:

> The future indwelling of the Holy Ghost in man amounts to a continuing incarnation of God.[271]

"Continuing incarnation" is an important phrase for Jung. What's the main point here? Jung is again highlighting what it means to psychologically develop from being contained to being a container. The religious task becomes, when we are containers, not worshiping God, but listening to what the Self is asking of us and then putting that into the world—facing the split in the Self, working to heal it, and then putting its "assignment" into the world. For Jung, that will be a new form of worship.[272] Note how much more responsibility he puts on the individual. He doesn't forget the danger of this new form of worship.

> The closer this bond becomes, the closer becomes the danger of a collision with evil because we are no longer protected from evil by dogma. We are living in intimate connection with our experience, and that experience can be good or bad.[273]

We have the basic idea of *Answer to Job* and its implications. There is a sequence of events: a collision with evil; a not succumbing; a holding to our integrity; the unconscious becoming creative; a line of

---

[270] *Answer to Job*, par. 692.
[271] Ibid., par 693.
[272] Edward Edinger's *The New God-Image* is a masterful study of Jung's late letters dealing with worship.
[273] *Answer to Job*, par. 593.

the development of life ensues; a new image of the Self appears (with its implications for our understanding of God); a new center of gravity is formed; a new life direction is shaped. This process happens because evil is faced in a particular way.

Victor the Russian Again

Careful consideration of Victor the Russian will add flesh to the paradigm under discussion. The reader may wish to review the earlier presentation of the dream on page 148.

> I see an ancient throne in a dimly lighted but large hallway.

Kings sit on thrones. Kings, psychologically speaking, represent the dominant value structure of a person, even of the times. Recall previous discussions. When we hear dreams such as this one of Victor the Russian out of context, they don't make sense, but when we carefully look at the imagery that make up the issue, then the pieces will start falling in place.

It is an ancient throne. This king has been around for a while.

> On the throne sits one who looks rugged and powerful, whose name (I think) is Victor.

Who is Victor? Or, asked differently, what is the psychology of victors? Power. The prevailing image of God is power, not love. Power is what is, in fact, moving us. Have you ever wondered why a so-called Christian society has produced so many wars and such greed? It is because the effect of our dominant value system is power. The "official" version is that God is Love; the real version is that far too often, God is power.

> When I first see him, I say to him, "You are the Russian." He gives me a laugh which conveys the impression that I have simply stated the obvious. I now learn that in order to survive down through the centuries (he has been around about two thousand years…

Two thousand years is the time of the Judeo-Christian God-image. Victor the Russian is an image of God, the *imago Dei* that has shaped two thousand years of Western history. It couldn't be more directly and accurately expressed.

> …about every hundred years or so he has had to find a new reincarnation. This is accomplished by someone, whom Victor selects, drinking a potion which Victor gives him. This person then becomes the new Victor the Russian, a sinister and powerful and dreaded person.

How does evil work? How does evil keep propagating itself? By visiting itself on somebody else, so that somebody else—perhaps beginning with a young child—will carry evil forward.

This is an image of abuse. There is a drive on the part of the God-image that this process repeats itself. Otherwise, it will die. It's a pretty horrible picture. But it is what is really driving historical events. The religion idealizes goodness, but the society it ordains is committed to violence. Recognize how perpetrators are driven to reproduce evil. Evil wants to continue itself.

Now, look at the dreamer's relationship to evil. This is where the dream gets interesting. Thus far, in sum, there is an image of a two-thousand-year-old king who is evil. That is the other side of the image of God that we don't want to acknowledge. That side is still effective in the way it creates behavior. This does not make logical sense, but when there is abuse, Victor the Russian is behind it.

What can we do about this state of affairs?

The dream continues:

> A friend of mine (whom I am unable to identify) takes the potion from Victor's hand and tries to give it to me to drink. I refuse it. He tries to force it on me, but I back away saying, I'll never drink it. Some of the potion spills out, and Victor takes the chalice back.

When someone unknown gives the dreamer Victor's poison, it means that the shadow of the dreamer "takes" the experience. The dreamer

175

is receiving the evil through an unknown reaction in himself. The dreamer says he is unable to identify the part of himself. This all happens unconsciously. We are not told who this unknown person is. I have a fantasy that this unknown person has to do with feeling guilty for having been victimized. The dream suggests the dreamer is unaware of how the guilt is instilled in him. A full awareness of the dreamer's relationship to this experience is not known at the time of the dream.

The dreamer doesn't accept this unknown relationship to the experience. He tries to fight it.

This is not exactly a Job experience because Job knew that his travail was coming from Satan and Yahweh. In the dream, there is a sort of "buffer" between the dreamer and evil. There has not been a direct confrontation with evil; the evil Victor works on him by way of an unconscious reaction. But this is a small detail. The main point is that evil is at work.

The dreamer is given the drink, not by Victor but by this unknown friend.

> He tries to force it on me, but I back away, saying I'll never drink it. Some of the potion spills out, and Victor takes the chalice back, saying it doesn't work anymore anyway. He then drinks it himself. Then the few people there turn to look at me and shrink back. The transition has taken place anyway in spite of my refusal of the chalice, and my features are apparently turning into those of the Russian.

The Russian offers the poison. The shadow takes it and tries to give it to the dreamer. The dreamer refuses. Victor drinks the poison. The dreamer turns into Victor the Russian anyway.

What should have happened? How do we keep the dreamer from becoming Victor the Russian? As I've reflected on the dream, I'd suggest he needs to accept the poison directly *but not drink it*. There is not a collision between the ego and the poison, between the ego and Victor. To accept the poison from Victor directly and to not drink it would be to say, "Yes, I have been victimized, and no, I am not responsible." As it is, the collision between evil and the ego does not occur consciously. In reality, I don't know whether the dreamer is accepting blame for some trauma earlier in his life or whether he is denying that anything happened back then. Possibly, either he has denied that it happened or he is blaming himself that something awful has happened to him. For our purposes, in light of *Answer to Job*, what is so powerful about the dream is that it shows how, when we are a victim of evil, and we don't respond in a protective way such as Jung has shown in *Answer to Job*, we too easily become the person who perpetuates the darkness into the next generation. That, I feel, is what the dream is trying to warn the dreamer about.

The result:

> I'm so angry that I begin beating on my "friend," who falls to the floor and is powerless to defend himself. He screams, and with both hands I pummel his body in my rage. The others do not dare to restrain me, but do try to aid my friend. There is a doctor who, between my blows, tried to administer an anesthetic to him.

At the time of the dream, the dreamer was in therapy with a therapist whose identity is unknown to me. Somehow I imagine that this therapist was a "feel good" therapist who took recourse in a kind of synthetic empathy. That is possibly where the therapy of the dreamer ran aground.

> I then cease hitting him, and within myself try to think how the awful power in me could be held in check. I come up with the idea that if a threat of an atomic bomb were held over my head, I would be stopped. The thought itself makes it seem that such is the case, that such an A-bomb is in readiness, and I begin to accept the fact that I must now bear the consequence of 'being' this Victor the Russian. I tie a kind of veil or turban around my head, and arise reluctantly to begin my new life.

I included the dream to show how this dark side of the God-image appears in a dream, how evil tries to propagate itself, and how we really can use the Book of Job as a model to accept the experience consciously but not take responsibility for it. In the dream, there is this intermediary reaction between the dreamer and his experience of

177

evil which could refer to either some way of denying it or falsely taking responsibility for it. That is how evil continues to propagate.

Finally, how to respond to these experiences is a matter of choice. If we do respond in a way that protects us, it *is* possible not to be infected by evil—to stop the buck with ourselves and to keep evil from repeating itself. Otherwise, the tendency of victims is to become the next perpetrator. *Answer to Job* is a help in the process of recognizing victimization, suffering consciously, not taking responsibility, and thereby stopping passing evil onto another person or another generation.

How could the dream have played out differently? I'd suggest the dreamer could have taken the vial and then poured it out. It's the act of taking it which says. "I acknowledge that I have been abused." Pouring it out would stipulate, "but I am not going to drink it"— meaning I am not responsible for having been abused. And I won't continue it on.

Ironically, it is saying, "I deserved this event," that sets the stage for passing it on. Either saying "It didn't happen" or "I deserved it" creates the condition of passing on harm. But if we can say, "it did happen, it is unjust, and I don't deserve it," that is the way to overcome becoming another perpetrator.

Here, the importance of the rage is paramount in acknowledging that this is an awful thing. Then the therapeutic job is helping that person live with that rage and helping them maintain their innocence until we can have the unconscious respond creatively in the way *Answer to Job* outlines. Then we can find a way through the experience. When the way is found through the suffering, I suggest that at least some of the rage will be mitigated. I'm not sure the rage ever goes away completely, but, I'm inclined to say, it can become manageable.

Reflections

Several phrases in Jung's major works are cornerstones of his opus. The notions all center around Jung's recognition and articulation of

178

the spirit. We've seen the true living spirit expressed in a variety of ways: as a teleological orientation anticipating our life's goal; as a foreshadowing of our life aim; as the call of individual destiny; as the controlling influence of the unconscious; as the forward-striving function of the unconscious; as the intelligent character of the unconscious; as what organizes our dreams and fantasies into a meaningful order (hence the capacity for our life to achieve the same). To that list, we can add Wisdom or Sophia, the presence which brings with her the capacity to initiate fundamental change at the core of our, and even our society's, values. This is one of the life lessons that Sophia can show us, and it is one of the assertions of The Book of Job to point us in her direction, as Jung never falters in honoring. This route to the destination of integrity, originality, and centering is pursued at a high cost. As we've seen, the Job model of the evolution of selfhood is not one that has to do with a hero's descent, or with a synthesis of endured opposites, or with an extraction out of the overpowering emotional messes. The critical juncture in the Book of Job is the moment when a suffering person stands up to the brutality of what has normatively been denied by their society as belonging to the sacred. The standing is with a clear and unmistakable clarity of the justice due to every human being simply by their birthright. This opens the door for Sophia and her spirit of guiding wisdom to enter into time and space and to become real in the lives of individuals and communities.

APPENDIX ONE

SELECTED HERO PARADIGMS DISCUSSED IN *SYMBOLS OF TRANSFORMATION*

HERO	CULTURE	PARAGRAPHS
RA	EGYPTIAN	351, 360, 451 – 458
OSIRIS	EGYPTIAN	349 – 374
MARDUK	BABYLON	375 – 379
GILGAMESH	AKKADIAN	396 – 398
MITHRAS	ROMAN	354, 396 – 398
CHRIST	CHRISTIAN	398
MUDJEKEEWIS/ HIAWATHA	AMERICAN	475 – 554
(Wagner's) SIEGMUND	GERMAN	555 – 571

APPENDIX TWO

FEMALE AUTHORS

Jungian books by women exploring the psychology and transformation of women.

Anne Baring and Jules Cashford, *The Myth of the Goddess: Evolution of an Image*

Jane Dallett, *Listening to the Rhino*

Linda Fierz-David, *Women's Dionysian Initiation, The Villa of Mysteries in Pompeii*

Barbara Hannah, *The Animus: The Spirit of Inner Truth in Women* (2 volumes)

Esther Harding, *Woman's Mysteries: Ancient & Modern*

Esther Harding, *The Way of All Women*

Emma Jung and Marie-Louise von Franz, *The Grail Legend*

Sylvia Brinton Perera, *Descent to the Goddess* *

Nancy Qualls-Corbett, *Awakening Woman* *

Nancy Qualls-Corbett, *The Sacred Prostitute* *

Marie-Louise von Franz, *Aurora Consurgens* *

Marie-Louise von Franz, *The Feminine in Fairy Tales*

Jane Wheelwright, *For Women Growing Older*

Diane Wolkstein and Samuel Noah Kramer, *Inanna, Queen of Heaven and Earth: Her Stories and Hymns from Sumer*

Marion Woodman, *Conscious Femininity* *

Marion Woodman, *The Pregnant Virgin* *

*These titles are available from Inner City Books at www.innercitybooks.net

APPENDIX THREE

DREAMS

The following are several dreams, as presented by the dreamer, that illustrate the themes we have discussed in Jung's major works.

SYMBOLS OF TRANSFORMATION

Jung's vision:

I see a gray rock face along which I sink into great depths. I stand in black dirt up to my ankles in a dark cave. Shadows sweep over me. I am seized by fear, but I know I must go in. I crawl through a narrow crack in the rock and reach an inner cave whose bottom is covered with black water. But beyond this I catch a glimpse of a luminous red stone which I must reach. I wade through the muddy water. The cave is full of the frightful noise of shrieking voices. I take the stone, it covers a dark opening in the rock. I hold the stone in my hand, peering around inquiringly. I do not want to listen to the voices, they keep me away. But I want to know. Here something wants to be uttered. I place my ear to the opening. I hear the flow of underground waters. I see the bloody head of a man on the dark stream. Someone wounded, someone slain floats there. I take in this image for a long time, shuddering. I see a large black scarab floating past on the dark stream. In the deepest reach of the stream shines a red sun, radiating through the dark water. There I see-and a terror seizes me-small serpents on the dark rock walls, striving toward the depths, where the sun shines. A thousand serpents crowd around, veiling the sun. Deep night falls. A red stream of blood, thick red blood springs up, surging for a long time, then ebbing. I am seized by fear. What did I see? (From C.G. Jung, *The Red Book*, p. 237; *Reader's Edition*, pp. 147f.)

I was with a youth in high mountains. It was before daybreak, the Eastern sky was already light. Then Siegfried's horn resounded over the mountains with a jubilant sound. We knew that our mortal enemy was coming. We were armed and lurked beside a narrow rocky path to murder him. Then we saw him coming high across the mountains on a chariot made of the bones of the dead. He drove boldly and magnificently over the steep rocks and

182

arrived at the narrow path where we waited in hiding. As he came around the turn ahead of us, we fired at the same time and he fell slain. Thereupon I turned to flee, and a terrible rain swept down. But after this I went through a torment unto death and I felt certain that I must kill myself if I could not solve the riddle of the murder of the hero. (From *The Red Book*, pp. 241f.; *Reader's Edition*, pp.160f.)

COMMENT: The incest theme is implied in the descent in the first paragraph. This descent preceded the depth of Jung's journey in his Red Book. The wounded hero is anticipated. It had to be killed, which we see in the next images which appears in Jung's vision. In the second part, which is a kind of prequel to the descent, we see Jung kill Siegfried. That hero figure Jung understood as "where there is a will there is a way." Siegfried, whose death made Jung's descent into the unconscious possible, would be parallel to Chiwantopel, who could not die and hence kept Miss Miller from her interior Self.

MYSTERIUM CONIUNCTIONIS, PART 1

Of a male:

There is a preparation for a film to be made. There is a disc which has pictures of all the characters to be in the film on it, and it is rotating in a counterclockwise direction. (The disc is like one of those viewmaster discs.) Then I realize that all the characters are being played by me, there are a dozen or more, both men and women. My image is being transformed into each character.

I then have a vision of my face being like a mask and being divided down the middle. On one half I am a man and on the other half I am a woman. Viewed from the side there is only one character presented, but viewed head-on there is a dual person.

COMMENT: The opposites in the dreamer's psyche are coming into awareness. Already a composite of inner fragments are cohering into a duality. Some synthesis has already occurred.

Of a female:

I dreamed I was taking water samples from deep pools, like wells. I had a special set of tools to use, a vial on a string with which to get the sample. I think my husband was there too. And at one point he told me to be sure to take a sample from the middle pool or to get the water from the middle. After I took the sample, I poured it into a cup.

COMMENT: The dreamer is finding her center, as a result of having also journeyed along the uncomfortable path of paying attention to the conflicts that were raging in herself.

MYSTERIUM PART 2

Of a female:

I am with several anonymous women whom I don't seem to know. We go downstairs in a strange house, and are confronted suddenly by some grotesque "ape-men" with evil faces dressed in fur with grey and black rings, with tails, horrible and leering. We are completely in their power, but suddenly I feel the only way we can save ourselves is not to panic and run or fight, but to treat these creatures with humanity as if to make them aware of their better side. So one of the ape-men comes up to me and I greet him like a dancing partner and begin to dance with him.

Later, I have been given supernatural healing powers and there is a man who is at death's door. I have a kind of quill or perhaps a bird's beak through which I blow air into his nostrils and he begins to breathe again. (From Joseph L. Henderson, Man and His Symbols, p. 138; paperback edition, p. 132.)

COMMENT: The "ape-men" are Adam figures, the dreamer is coming into awareness of the raw instinctual energies within. This, in turn, breathes life into her existence.

Of a female:

A woman dreamed that she went into an underground cavern that was divided into rooms containing stills and other mysterious-looking chemical apparatus. Two scientists were working over the final process of a prolonged series of experiments, which they hoped to bring to a successful conclusion with her help. The end product was to be in the form of golden crystals, which were to be separated from the mother liquid resulting from the many previous solutions and distillations. While the chemists worked over the vessel, the dreamer and her lover lay together in an adjoining room, their sexual embrace supplying the energy essential for the crystallization of the priceless golden substance. (From Edward Edinger, *Anatomy of the Psyche,* p. 218, quoting Esther Harding, *Psychic Energy: Its Source and Goal*, pp. 453f.)

COMMENT: The polarity has been constellated and is beginning the process of synthesis, the unity of the dreamer's personality.

AION

Of a female:

I am in a large building like a museum or a hotel. There are lots of tanks of goldfish in different rooms. Some of the tanks get broken. There is a lot of water and glass and fish on the floor. I know I can't save all the fish, so I pick up one large one, about 14 inches long, gold, like a perch, and carry it in my arms like a baby to try to find one of the other tanks to put it in. But I can't find any other tanks. I sense a communication with the fish. It's like I can understand what it is thinking. It communicates that it can live for a fairly long time out of water. I finally find a plastic bag and put some water in it and put this fish in it until I can find something better.

COMMENT: The religious container has broken, and the dreamer must find another way to connect with the contents once available to her.

Of a female:

Several people have agreed to travel to spend time together in a large house. My brother has agreed to be there early to take care of a special fish that we will transport to a body of water when we are all there. We get a call that the fish is in trouble, and my brother has been called away and cannot stay to take care of it.

When I get there, other people are already there. I see the fish in a large sun room on the floor. The fish is large and chunky. There is no water to put him in. There is some sense that the water he was in was toxic, and he is actually better out of the water. He scoots about on the floor. He

185

scoots toward me, looking at me with soulful eyes, wanting something from me. I don't know how to help him. [abridged]

COMMENT: Another broken religious container.

Of a female:

I am with other women and there is something about a dinner. There are fish on a plate. I am having a déjà vu about seeing the fish before. It is lying on a plate and suddenly jumps at my right arm, grabbing me with its teeth. I grab at his body trying to pull him off me. The pain awakens me and I realize that I am digging into my arm with my own fingernails!

COMMENT: In fact, in due course after the dream, the dreamer found herself in an overwhelmingly powerful emotional experience. That would be the "first" fish as we talked about the two meanings of the fish. The fruit of accepting that experience and also watching how it evolved, gave birth to her own creativity, which was anticipated in the second dream of the same night as the previous dream:

I am walking to breakfast. There is a man in front of me. He walks up this gradual incline onto a glass "bridge." I follow him. It is in the breakfast room. The room has places to sit on the left and the right below, but the Bridge has only one table in the center, middle of the bridge. It is enclosed by glass on the sides and the bottom so that I can view the entire room. It is finished with beautiful wood at the outer edges of the floor. It matches the trim that edges the floor and ceiling of the full room. There are windows viewing the eastern and western sky. The sun is rising in the east-northeast.

The man will sit facing north, and I am invited to sit across from him facing south. He will be able to "watch my back" to the north and I will be able to view the other three directions.

COMMENT: It's no accident that the fish grabbed hold of the dreamer's *arm*. That arm is the arm of her creative work, and that creative work is symbolized by the man she follows, her internal creative spirit that guides her in this regard (the second fish born out of the first fish of an overwhelming emotional experience). He opens

186

new vistas for her and will, indeed, watch her back, i.e., become the link between her and the unknown. In that sense, the dream is about a new day symbolized by the breakfast.

These two dreams of the same night required a psychological journey of more than ten years until their final and full realization was accomplished and brought into life.

Of a woman:

> In place of the street signs which had been abolished, posters had been set up on every street corner, proclaiming in white letters on a black background the twenty words people were not permitted to say. The first was "Lord"—to be on the safe side I must have dreamt it in English. I don't recall the following words and possibly didn't even dream them. But the last one was "I." (From Charlotte Beradt, *The Third Reich of Dreams*, p. 23.)

COMMENT: The dream was collected, and eventually published, by a German woman just at the time Hitler was coming to power. The connection between the God-image and the integrity of the individual could not be more clearly portrayed.

APPENDIX FOUR

EDWARD F. EDINGER'S STUDY GUIDES

Symbols of Transformation

Edward F. Edinger, *Transformation of Libido: A Seminar on C.G. Jung's* Symbols of Transformation
(Also available from the Los Angeles Jung Institute's C.G. Jung Bookstore)

Mysterium Coniunctionis

Edward F. Edinger, *The Mysterium Lectures**

Edward F. Edinger, *The Mystery of the Coniunctio**
(A study of *Psychology of the Transference, Collected Works*, vol. 16, but Edinger's work sheds light in a readable way on the nature of alchemy)

Aion

Edward F. Edinger, *The Aion Lectures**

Answer to Job

Edward F. Edinger, *Transformation of the God-Image**

Edward F. Edinger, *Encounter With the Self: A Jungian Commentary on William Blake's Illustrations of the Book of Job* *
(A study of William Blake's illustrations)

Edward F. Edinger, *The New God-Image*
(A study of Jung's "theology" extracted from Jung's letters, a useful addition to Jung's reflections on religion in *Answer to Job*)

*These titles are available from Inner City Books at www.innercitybooks.net

BIBLIOGRAPHY

The 5th Dimension. "Aquarius/Let the Sun Shine In." Single from The Age of Aquarius. Soul City, 1969.

"The Allegory of Merlin." The Alchemy Website. http://www.levity.com/alchemy/merlin.html.

Edinger, Edward F. *The Aion Lectures*. Edited by Deborah Wesley. Toronto: Inner City Books, 1996.

_____. *Archetype of the Apocalypse: A Jungian Study of the Book of Revelation*. Edited by George R. Elder. Chicago: Open Court, 1999.

_____. *The Bible and the Psyche*. Toronto: Inner City Books, 1986.

_____. *The Mysterium Lectures*. Edited by Joan Dexter Blackmer. Toronto: Inner City Books, 1995.

_____. *The New God-Image: A Study of Jung's Key Letters Concerning the Evolution of the Western God-Image*. Edited by Dianne D. Cordic and Charles Yates. Wilmette, IL: Chiron Publications, 1996.

_____. *Transformation of the God-Image: An Elucidation of Jung's Answer to Job*. Edited by Lawrence W. Jaffe. Toronto: Inner City Books, 1992.

Hannah, Barbara. *Jung: His Life and Work: A Biographical Memoir*. New York: G.P. Putnam's Sons, 1976.

Johnson, Robert A. *Inner Work: Using Dreams and Active Imagination for Personal Growth*. San Francisco: Harper and Row, 1986.

Jung, C.G. *Analytical Psychology: Notes of the Seminar Given in 1925* (Bollingen Series XCIX). Edited by William McGuire. Princeton: Princeton University Press, 1989.

_____. *Answer to Job.* (From Vol. 11 of the *Collected Works of C. G. Jung,* Jung Extracts, 33) Translated by R.F.C. Hull. Princeton: Princeton University Press, 2010.

_____. *C.G. Jung Speaking: Interviews and Encounters* (Bollingen Series XCVII). Edited by William McGuire and R.F.C. Hull. Princeton: Princeton University Press, 1977.

_____. *The Collected Works* (Bollingen Series XX). 20 vols. Edited by H. Read, M. Fordham, G. Adler, William McGuire. Translated by R.F.C. Hull. Princeton: Princeton University Press, 1953-1979.

_____. *Dream Analysis: Notes of the Seminar Given in 1928-1930* (Bollingen Series XCIX). Edited by William McGuire. Princeton: Princeton University Press, 1984.

_____. *Memories, Dreams, Reflections.* Edited by Aniela Jaffé. Translated by Richard and Clara Winston. New York: Vintage Books, 1965.

Jung, Carl and Pauli, Wolfgang. *Atom and Archetype: The Pauli/Jung Letters, 1932-1958.* Edited by C.A. Meier. Translated by David Roscoe. Princeton, Princeton University Press, 2001.

Wikipedia. "George Ripley (alchemist)". Last modified July 9, 2022. https://en.wikipedia.org/wiki/George_Ripley_(alchemist).

Wikipedia. "Gerhard Dorn." Last modified January 22, 2022. https://en.wikipedia.org/wiki/Gerhard_Dorn.

Wikipedia. "Ibn Umayl." Last modified August 12, 2022. https://en.wikipedia.org/wiki/Ibn_Umayl.

Wikipedia. "Identification with the Aggressor." Last modified July 12, 2022. https://en.wikipedia.org/wiki/Identification_with_the_Aggressor.

Wikipedia. "Stockholm Syndrome." Last modified August 28, 2022. https://en.wikipedia.org/wiki/Stockholm_syndrome.

van der Kolk, Bessel. *The Body Keeps the Score: Brain, Mind, and Body in the Healing of Trauma.* New York: Penguin Random House, 2014.

von Franz, Marie-Louise. *C.G. Jung: His Myth in Our Time.* Translated by William H. Kennedy. Toronto: Inner City Books, 1998.

_____. *Number and Time: Reflections Leading toward a Unification of Depth Psychology and Physics.* Translated by Andrea Dykes. Evanston: Northwestern University Press, 1974.

Studies in Jungian Psychology
by Jungian Analysts
Quality Paperbacks

Prices and payment in $US (except in Canada, $Cdn)

Risky Business: Environmental Disasters and the Nature Archetype
Stephen J. Foster (Boulder, CO) ISBN 9781894574334. 128 pp. $25

The Mysterium Lectures
Edward F. Edinger ISBN 9780919123663. 352 pp. $40

The Mystery of the Coniunctio
Edward Edinger ISBN 9780919123670. 112 pp. $25

Transformation of the God-Image
Edward F. Edinger ISBN 9780919123557. 144pp. $25

Encounter With the Self
Edward F. Edinger ISBN 9780919123212. 80pp $25

The Sacred Psyche: A Psychological Approach to the Psalms
Edward F. Edinger ISBN 9781894574099. 160 pp. $25

Jung and Yoga: The Psyche-Body Connection
Judith Harris (London, Ontario) ISBN 9780919123953. 160 pp. $25

Descent to the Goddess: A Way of Initiation for Women
Sylvia Brinton Perera (New York) ISBN 9780919123052. 112 pp. $25

The Illness That We Are: A Jungian Critique of Christianity
John P. Dourley (Ottawa) ISBN 978091912318. 128 pp. $25

Coming To Age: The Croning Years and Late-Life Transformation
Jane R. Prétat (Providence) ISBN 9780919123632. 144 pp. $25

Jungian Dream Interpretation: A Handbook of Theory and Practice
James A. Hall, M.D. (Dallas) ISBN 9780919123120. 128 pp. $25

Aurora Consurgens
Marie-Louise von Franz ISBN 9780919123908 576 pp. $50

The Sacred Prostitute: Eternal Aspect of the Feminine
Nancy Qualls-Corbett (Birmingham) ISBN 9780919123311. 176 pp. $30

Awakening Woman
Nancy Qualls-Corbett (Birmingham) ISBN 9781894574020. 160 pp. $25

Addiction to Perfection: The Still Unravished Bride
Marion Woodman (Toronto) ISBN 9780919123113. 208 pp. $30/$35hc

The Pregnant Virgin: A Process of Psychological Development
Marion Woodman (Toronto) ISBN 9780919123205. 208 pp. $30pb/$35hc

Conscious Femininity: Interviews with Marion Woodman
Introduction by Marion Woodman ISBN 9780919123595. 160 pp. $25

INNER CITY BOOKS
21 Milroy Crescent Toronto, ON M1C 4B6 Canada
416-927-0355
www.innercitybooks.net